SOFT JEWELRY

HOW TO SEW JEWELRY

by Judith Conaway

SIMON AND SCHUSTER • NEW YORK

PUBLISHED BY SIMON AND SCHUSTER
A DIVISION OF GULF & WESTERN CORPORATION
SIMON & SCHUSTER BUILDING
ROCKEFELLER CENTER
1230 AVENUE OF THE AMERICAS
NEW YORK, NEW YORK 10020

DESIGNED BY EVE METZ
MANUFACTURED IN THE UNITED STATES OF AMERICA

1 2 3 4 5 6 7 8 9 10

LIBRARY OF CONGRESS CATALOGING IN PUBLICATION DATA

CONAWAY, JUDITH, DATE.
    SOFT JEWELRY.

    BIBLIOGRAPHY: P.
    INCLUDES INDEX.
    1. JEWELRY MAKING—AMATEURS' MANUALS.
2. TEXTILE CRAFTS. I. TITLE.
TT212.C64   746.9′2   78-17047
ISBN 0-671-24122-2

Photographs by Jim Robertson.
Drawings by Judith Conaway and Chloris Noelke.
All objects in this book were designed and worked by the author
unless otherwise credited.

ACKNOWLEDGMENTS

It would have been impossible to put this book together without the help of a great many friends. Valjean McLenighan, Mary Robey, Irene Rada-kovik, Russell Patterson and Stuart Klawans all subjected themselves to the discomfort of the hot lights so I could photograph their hands. My sister, Janelle Conaway, helped with some of the typing.

Jim Robertson, who did most of the photography, and Chloris Noelke, who helped with the drawings, deserve my special thanks. Chloris's enthusiasm for this project and expertise in design, needlework and re-lated fields have contributed in many subtle ways to this book. Chloris lent us her apartment with its fascinating antiques and collections to use as a setting for many of our photos. She also modeled some of the jewelry. The other models were Maria Callejo, Sue Cigan and Flora Noelke. The painting in some of the pictures is a work in progress by David LeBoy.

As always, of course, I owe thanks to Stuart Klawans for his constant personal support.

FOR MY MOTHER, MIRIAM SWANSON CONAWAY,
WHO TAUGHT ME TO EMBROIDER AND SEW

Contents

SOFT JEWELRY

Introduction

A PIECE OF JEWELRY is an accessory. Its function is to enhance the face, hair, body and costume of the wearer. But jewelry is not merely decorative. Jewels are not just accessories, they are accessories that have value.

One reason jewelry has value is that it confers power. Perhaps jewelry had its origin in the talismans made by primitive peoples, designed to ward off evil spirits, enchant animals or cure toothaches. The adornments of the tribal witch doctor were intended to set their wearer apart, give him a mysterious identity and mesmerize the viewer—functions still performed by jewelry today.

In many tribal societies, adornments indicate status, family, marital state or personal achievements. A well-known example of this is the headdress of the American Indian, to which feathers and other decorations were added as rewards for bravery or skill. The gold braid and ribbons worn by military personnel offer another example of earned adornments. Our culture, too, uses jewelry symbolically. The wedding ring is the most obvious example.

In more complex societies jewelry has value as a sign of wealth. The very word "jewelry" connotes luxury. Fine jewelry is crafted from the rarest materials—gold, silver, diamonds, emeralds and other precious metals and stones—and worked with skill and attention to detail.

Needle-made jewelry is no exception. The most precious pieces are fashioned from the finest available cloths and threads and worked in tiny, perfect stitches. Among the most beautiful of these objects are the embroidered silk bags, collars, cuffs, fans and belts of Imperial China. Each delicately colored piece is trimmed with handmade braids and tassels.

Few of us will ever achieve the level of technical skill shown

Cheyenne medicine necklace. The small pouches were used for storing herbs. (Photograph courtesy Field Museum, Chicago.)

by the needleworkers of the past. But then, few of us will ever go blind making lace or embroidering handkerchiefs for a few pennies a day, as was the lot of many women who could support themselves only through piecework sewing. Nor are we forced to do needlework because it is proper. The fact that so many women—and an increasing number of men—do needlework today is a testimony to the rewards of the craft. Perhaps the greatest reward is the creation of beautiful, valuable objects for gifts or for yourself.

This book will show you how to use your needlework skills to

Herbert Walker, a Cheyenne Indian. Walker's costume displays many sewing techniques: wrapping, braiding, appliqué, leatherwork, featherwork and beading. (Photograph courtesy Field Museum, Chicago.)

Chinese cases for mirrors, cosmetics, herbs, money and spectacles. Embroidered and appliquéd in cream, peacock-blue and gold on black silk. (Photograph courtesy Field Museum, Chicago.)

make exquisite jewelry. I have tried to plan the book to help all kinds of needleworkers, from beginners to professionals. If you are just starting out in needlework, you will want to practice each technique before you use it in a final piece.

Most readers, however, have had some experience with at least one sewing technique, since sewing is still considered a proper occupation for women, and the teaching of some techniques survives in our high-school home economics classes. You will probably want to use a familiar technique for your first jewelry project. The Index of Techniques on page 185 will help you select your project.

Making jewelry is also a delightful way to get acquainted with a new technique. The Index of Techniques can help you plan a crafts course for yourself.

If you are an experienced needleworker, you will find all the projects in this book quite easy. In fact, by now you may have looked at all the pictures and have had a great many ideas of your own. But even though the jewelry you want to make may not resemble mine, I think you will benefit by reading some of the instructions.

This display of beaded and sewn objects from Ghana provides a wealth of design motifs and ideas. Coils, stars, triangles, diamonds, concentric circles and nets are universal textile motifs. Even more direct information might come from studying the shapes of the bags and hats. (Photograph courtesy Field Museum, Chicago.)

SOFT JEWELRY AS GIFTS AND FOR SALE

Small hand-crafted objects are among those most easily sold at crafts fairs, church bazaars and other such events. On page 183, you will find a listing of the projects in this book by level of difficulty. The simpler projects are ideal for selling purposes. Studying the step-by-step directions will help you plan production more efficiently.

Your finest needle-made jewelry, however, will not be made for sale but for your personal use. A hand-embroidered bag is a luxurious gift. A feather necklace can transform an old dress. The needleworker has the means of creating just the right jewelry, the rich details that make a wardrobe both elegant and individual.

SOME GENERAL RULES

1. Read the instructions. You might as well learn from my mistakes as from your own.

2. Take your time and do it right. No matter what your sewing experience, you are going to encounter some problems in learning to sew jewelry. The most elegant materials are sometimes the most difficult to handle. Get used to the idea that you must learn by trial and error. If you sew a seam wrong, don't rip it apart. Work the stitches out carefully and do it over. Analyze what you did wrong the first time. In the long run, taking your time is worth it. Suddenly you will find yourself able to tackle any project, plan it with common sense and execute it as if you were a fine guild craftsman. Then you will be ready to design jewelry yourself.

3. Pay attention to details. They are what make the difference between mere ornament and real jewelry, in whatever medium the jewelry is worked. That is why I have devoted so much space in this book to discussions of interfacings, linings, cords, trims and closures.

4. Use the best available materials. Your hours of labor are valuable. Don't waste them by using cheap synthetic fabrics or threads. Leave these inferior materials to mass production. In this book you will find a strong prejudice toward—in fact, an insistence upon—natural materials: silk, linen and cotton. You can afford these materials even though they cost more. You might pay six dollars for a yard of silk and two dollars for the same amount of "100 per cent polyester." But four dollars is a small price for the enormous difference in the quality—and the value—of the final piece.

1 · Designing Needle-made Jewelry

MOST PEOPLE THINK of designing as sitting down in front of a large blank paper, thinking of a form, and drawing what the form will look like. In crafts, however, designing also means handling the materials, experimenting with techniques and working up samples. Designing is done with the hands as well as the head.

The design of a piece of jewelry is dependent on the techniques you use. For example, there are certain three-dimensional effects that you can create with needle lace but not with batik.

Most of this book is about materials and techniques. The instructions show you how to use certain stitches on certain fabrics for certain results. Doing the projects will help train your design sense through your hands. This chapter is concerned with your head—your understanding of some basic elements of design.

In the pages that follow, I will review some principles of balance, shape, color and texture, and show how they relate to each other in a design. The jewelry designer must also consider another element—the wearer. The shapes in the design must enhance the shapes of the wearer's face and figure; colors in the piece must harmonize with the wearer's skin, hair and eye coloring.

The Jewelry Designer's Check List on pages 30 to 33 will help you apply the principles of balance, shape, color and texture to the design of jewelry for a specific wearer.

BALANCE

The most common symbol of balance is the weight scale, which works on the same principle as a seesaw. In both, a flat plane called a *lever* is balanced on a point, the *fulcrum*. The weights on each end of the lever must be equal to keep the lever horizontal. The scale is kept horizontal by the force of gravity, which pulls with equal force on objects of equal weight.

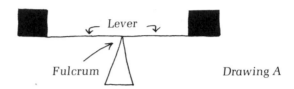

Drawing A

Our sense of visual balance is related to our perception of ourselves. Humans instinctively perceive themselves as standing up, defying the law of gravity. Our feeling that we are "in balance" when we are standing up straight manifests itself visually in our strong preference for the vertical over the horizontal line. The two lines in Drawing B are exactly the same length. But the vertical line appears longer.

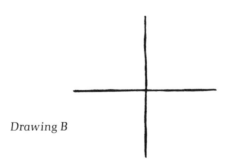

Drawing B

When people look at you, they see you as a vertical line. But the degree of verticality they perceive depends on how wide you are. A thin person looks slightly taller than a fat person of the same height. If you want to look slimmer than you really are, you must create a strong vertical line to balance the horizontal lines of your eyes, shoulders, waist, hips and feet.

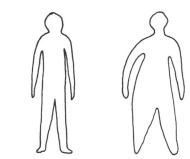

Drawing C

I don't mean that all overweight people should wear clothes with stripes down the center. The human preference for the vertical is so strong that only suggestions of verticality are needed. Look at Drawing D. The vertical line created by the woman's belt buckle and necklace focuses the eye just as effectively, and much more subtly, than does the vertical line created by the center stripe.

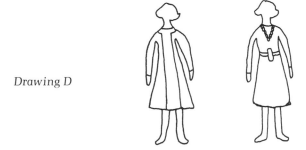

Drawing D

Whenever you look at something, your eyes focus on a spot within that object. In Drawings A and B, your eye focuses automatically on the point where the vertical line intersects the horizontal one. The point where your eyes focus is the central point of your vision, the "fulcrum" on which you will then seek visual balance. In designing jewelry, you can direct your viewer's eye toward a point of focus of your choosing.

If you balance the elements in a design properly, you will direct the viewer's eye toward a central balance point. If you think you have no sense of visual balance, remember the seesaw feats of your childhood and translate what you learned into visual terms. Drawing E shows how the principles of balance apply both to a seesaw and to an imaginary piece of jewelry, an oval pendant. In each drawing, visual balance is achieved around a central point. The drawing shows why we can speak of forms as having "weight" or "mass."

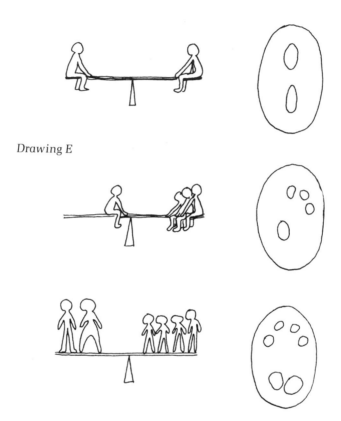

Drawing E

SHAPE

When we look at the world, we see distinct forms, which we perceive as having weight, mass and shape. A form's shape narrows our vision. Our eyes first focus on the shape, and then on a point within that shape.

Every shape directs our eyes toward a focal point. Some shapes, such as squares, circles and hexagons, direct our eyes toward their centers. Other shapes, such as trapezoids and triangles, direct our eyes outside themselves. Ovals, rectangles and diamonds direct our eyes toward their narrow ends.

You can use this knowledge of shapes to direct the viewer's eye toward your best features and away from your worst ones. You can also use shapes to achieve a pleasing visual balance in your appearance.

Let's say that you are of medium height and weight, with a

The feathered nest pendant serves as a buckle on a thin leather belt. Instructions for making the pendant are on page 97. Notice how the shape of a belt can change the impression the model's figure makes.

A quilted silk cummerbund gives the dress an entirely different look.
Instructions for making this cummerbund start on page 139.

small bustline and large hips. The effect is bottom heavy; your design problem is to restore the visual balance. You could design a striking collar that directed attention to the upper half of your body. The angle of the collar could direct attention up even further to your face. Add a striking hat and the viewer's eye will be focused on a point as far away as possible from the offending hips, as illustrated in Drawing F.

Drawing F

COLOR

We can't achieve visual balance without understanding color, because color is the way we see light, and without light we couldn't see anything at all.

Direct light from the sun appears white. But it is actually made up of all colors. In a rainbow, millions of tiny drops of water bend the sun's white rays and separate them into bands according to their length. We see each band as a different color. All humans who are not color-blind can see six distinct bands in a rainbow: red, orange, yellow, green, blue and violet.

If you look more closely at a rainbow, you can see that these bands of color are not really distinct. The bands seem to overlap each other—in fact, three of the six colors are formed by the overlapping of rays from other bands. Orange is partly red and partly yellow. Green is partly yellow and partly blue. Violet is partly blue and partly red. We call red, yellow and blue *primary colors*. We call orange, green and violet *secondary colors*.

A longer study of the rainbow reveals even more distinguishable colors. *Intermediate colors* appear between the primary and secondary colors. In a rainbow, then, we can distinguish twelve colors: red, red-orange, orange, yellow-orange, yellow, yellow-green, green, blue-green, blue, blue-violet, violet and red-violet.

When light strikes a surface, it is either reflected or absorbed. Everything that has color contains chemicals called *pigments*, which absorb some light rays and reflect others back to the viewer's eye. Your red dress contains pigments that absorb all the light waves except the red ones, which bounce back to your eye and are perceived as red.

The eye also registers black and white, which are not really colors. White is the reflection of all the colors at once. Black is the absence of color—a black surface absorbs all the light rays and reflects none.

When you change the color of a costume, you are actually

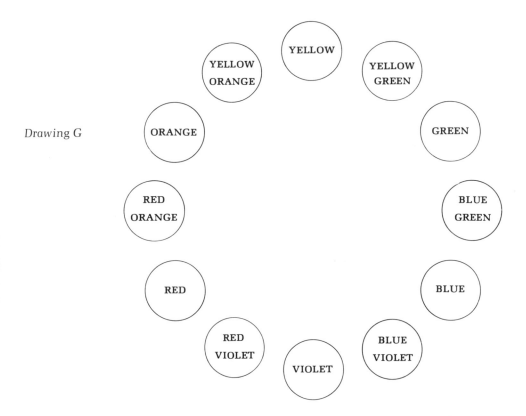

Drawing G

changing the quality of light reflected to the viewer. In the viewer's eye, the colors play upon each other and balance each other. The art of combining colors is not matching one color to another but achieving a pleasing interplay of light against light.

Fortunately, there are some simple principles to guide us in achieving color balance. To apply the principles, you will need a tool called a *color wheel*. A color wheel contains the twelve distinguishable rainbow colors arranged in a circle. The wheel does not contain every color, but it is a tool for measuring the relationships between all colors.

You can buy a color wheel at an art supply store. Grumbacher, a leading manufacturer of artists' pigments, publishes a Color Computer—a color wheel that shows all the possible mixes of colors on the wheel. You can also copy the color wheel in Drawing G and color it with crayons. If you are unsure of your color sense, you will find it helpful to have a color wheel next to you as you read the paragraphs that follow.

When you look at a color wheel, your eye will be drawn irresistibly to the yellow color band. If you turn the color wheel so that yellow is at the top, the other colors will be arranged in descending order of intensity. The closer a color is to yellow, the brighter it looks. The closer a color is to violet, which is opposite yellow, the darker that color looks. You are observing the difference in color *value*. You can balance color values just as you can balance weight values.

Black and white can also be said to have values. We see the intermediate values as shades of gray.

The principle for balancing color values can be stated very simply: The lighter a color's value, the more the color will advance toward the viewer; the darker a color's value, the more it will recede from the viewer.

Color values affect the visual weights of the objects that you see. If you wear a dark dress, you look smaller than if you wear a light dress. If you wear a yellow blouse and a blue skirt, the viewer's eyes will be directed toward the blouse. If you wear a blue blouse and a yellow skirt, you will focus the viewer's attention on the skirt.

Let's go back to the design problem illustrated in Drawing D. Another way the woman could balance her costume would be to wear dark colors on her wide hips and light colors on top. Or she might create a strong vertical line with a light color against a dark background. Colors and shapes affect each other.

COLOR HARMONIES

Most of us were taught that certain colors "matched" and others did not, and we learned to dress according to those rules. But this method of choosing colors is far from foolproof. Once on a bus I sat across from a woman who was wearing an extremely expensive suit knitted in a black-and-white diamond pattern. Every detail of her costume matched the suit. Her hat was a beret composed of black-and-white triangles. The frames of her glasses were black with little white diamond-shaped inserts. Her earrings were a dangling profusion of black-and-white beads, and of course she had on a necklace and bracelet to match. Her purse was of black patent leather. She even wore black stockings that had a diamond pattern and carried a black-and-white umbrella. The pathetic thing was that she must have spent hours looking for just the right accessories for that suit.

The woman on the bus did not understand that color is reflected light. Colors literally vibrate at your eye—and their vibrations affect each other.

Although there are no rules for color matching, there are general principles that govern color harmony, which is an entirely different thing. The colors on the color wheel are notations of light waves, just as musical notes are notations of sound waves. The color red can't be matched any more than middle C can. But, like notes, colors can flow into each other, clash, and otherwise affect each other's quality.

Principle 1. Colors next to each other on the color wheel tend to blend into each other. Yellow and yellow-green share many common rays; they are literally "on the same wave lengths." So there is a minimum amount of vibration at the point where these two colors meet.

You can use this principle to bridge the visual gaps between the colors in a costume. If you have orange-red hair and want to wear a purple dress, you might create too startling a contrast. You can soften the contrast by wearing a collar or necklace in shades or combinations of red-violet, red and red-orange.

Principle 2. Colors opposite each other on the color wheel intensify each other. A yellow dot embroidered on a violet background will appear yellower than it will against a green background. Principle 2 was flagrantly violated by the perfectly matched woman on the bus. Black and white function as opposites—they vibrate against each other. Try staring at a chessboard for a few minutes and you will see what I mean.

Using opposite, or *complementary,* colors is not always a mistake. Sometimes intensification of colors is just the effect you want. Rosy-skinned women with light-brown hair and blue eyes look especially good in shades of violet. The violet intensifies the blondeness of their hair and reflects the blue of the eyes. In this case, the woman is applying both Principle 1 and Principle 2. Similarly, auburn-haired women instinctively wear green when they want to show off their hair. Red and green are opposites, or *complements,* on the color wheel.

Principle 3. Colors that are neither opposite each other nor next to each other on the color wheel will appear to move toward each other's opposites. A yellow-orange form embroidered on a blue-green background will appear to have reddish tones, since red-orange is the opposite of blue-green. A red-violet form on a yellow-orange background will move toward the violet part of the wheel—it will appear bluer to the viewer.

Let's apply Principle 3 to a specific design problem. You have a yellow-green blouse and a pinkish complexion. The effect is bilious. Since pink is a tint of red, find red on the color wheel. The yellow-green is pushing the red in your skin toward the violets on the wheel. You are dangerously close to the vibrating effect caused by complementary colors, and in this case, you don't want to intensify either your pinkish/purple skin or your blouse. Your object, then, will be to move your skin tone away from the violets and toward the oranges. To harmonize the blouse with your face, you would choose blue-green, blue or blue-violet, colors that are opposite the oranges on the color wheel.

Very few people, of course, have skin that is pink. Most human skins are brown. Brown is composed of all three primary colors—red, blue and yellow. So your skin color is actually the reflection of many colors at once. So-called white skin contains few pigments. Most light rays bounce right off the surface of your skin. So-called black skin absorbs most of the light that falls on it.

But though skin tones are lightened or darkened by the presence or absence of pigments, all brown skins reflect red, blue and yellow rays. Some brown skins appear distinctly yellow in tone—they reflect more yellow rays than red or blue ones. Very dark-brown skin can have a slightly blue cast. American Indian skin is dark brown with a slightly red cast.

Brown hair, too, will tend to be reddish, yellowish or bluish. If you have "dishwater blonde" hair, you've probably noticed that it turns slightly green or slightly orange in the sun.

If you can look in a mirror and identify a color cast in your hair or skin, it will be easy for you to use the color wheel. If you have reddish-brown hair and want to make it appear redder, you would choose colors opposite the reds on the color wheel—greens. Wearing violet would move the red in your hair back toward the yellow—in other words, it would make your hair appear less red.

If your hair and skin appear just plain brown, they probably have about equal amounts of red, blue and yellow. You can change the color of your hair to make it appear to have reddish or yellowish tones, simply by choosing opposites of red or yellow on the color wheel.

The Jewelry Designer's Check List on pages 30 to 33 gives specific suggestions for different skin-hair-eye combinations. Your best colors are those that combine with your coloring to create the maximum pleasing effect on the viewer.

TEXTURES

The texture of a surface affects both its color and its form, since texture affects the way a surface reflects light. The principles of texture can be stated very simply. The smoother a texture, the more it will reflect light; therefore, the brighter the object will seem to appear. The rougher the texture, the less it will reflect light; therefore, the darker the object will seem to appear.

Textures also have weight. Sometimes the weight is physical— a rough tweed actually weighs more per yard than does a silk chiffon. But textures can have visual weight as well. A nubby-textured white sweater will appear larger than a smooth-textured white sweater.

In any design, you must balance shape, color and texture to achieve pleasing results. You can create visual balance by contrasting or blending colors, by proper placement of shapes, and by using appropriate textures. The best designers take all these elements into account—and achieve amazing optical illusions.

JEWELRY DESIGNER'S CHECK LIST

Now that you've reviewed some principles of design, you are ready to apply them to specific jewelry pieces. This check list emphasizes the most important design element in jewelry—the wearer. To use the check list, just observe the person for whom you are designing the jewelry and check off the appropriate descriptions. The check list will give you some general guidelines for making a piece of jewelry that is functional—in other words, flattering.

Jewelry Designer's Check List

WEARER'S FIGURE

Short and slim

Suggested shapes: Vertical lines to add height, round and ruffled shapes to soften lines. Avoid overemphasizing head and shoulders. Wear smallish shapes for proportion.

Suggested colors: Avoid cutting figure in half with too much contrast between upper and lower halves. Medium to light colors add visual weight.

Suggested textures: Anything goes, except outsized brocades or patterns.

SHORT AND PLUMP

Suggested shapes: Vertical lines to add height. Soft, thin belts only. Keep shapes small for proportion.

Suggested colors: Dark to medium shades; light shades in vertical center of figure. Avoid outlining shoulders, bust or hips with color.

Suggested textures: Medium-weight, fairly smooth textures. Avoid bulky wools or overly delicate laces.

MEDIUM AND SLIM

Suggested shapes: Anything that emphasizes wearer's best features.

Suggested colors: Bright or light colors near wearer's best features.

Suggested textures: Medium-weight fabrics in all textures. Look for patterns that are neither too small nor too large. Smooth, shiny fabrics should be near wearer's best features.

MEDIUM AND PLUMP

Suggested shapes: Vertical lines to detract from width. Wide V-shapes and other shapes that direct eye toward face. Avoid large belts, purses, collars. Too-small shapes will accentuate girth by contrast.

Suggested colors: Dark to medium shades, with lighter colors as accents. Avoid cutting figure in half with too much contrast between upper and lower halves.

Suggested textures: Avoid overly shiny or overly rough fabrics. Choose medium weights and textures.

TALL AND SLIM

Suggested shapes: Anything that emphasizes wearer's best features. Excessive slimness can be countered by horizontal lines. Avoid tiny accessories.

Suggested colors: Anything that flatters.

Suggested textures: Anything that flatters.

TALL AND PLUMP

Suggested shapes: Vertical lines to counteract width. Avoid too-large head wraps or hats with wide brims. Avoid tiny accessories. Wear large, long shapes.

Suggested colors: Dark to medium tones. Use light and bright colors only as accents.

Suggested textures: Avoid overly thin or overly bulky fabrics.

WEARER'S FACE

SQUARE

Suggested shapes: Round, ruffly shapes in asymmetrical forms to soften jaw. Draped cords or soft scarves to lessen angularity. Avoid long earrings that attract eye to jaw level.

ROUND

Suggested shapes: Direct attention to upper half of head with bulky head wraps. Wear V-shaped collars or long, V-shaped necklaces to counteract roundness. Lengthen neck by wearing deep necklines. Avoid chokers.

OVAL

Suggested shapes: Anything goes. Wear closely wrapped head coverings, eccentric earrings, scarves, chokers.

TRIANGULAR

Suggested shapes: Wear chokers, long earrings to add fullness at jaw level.

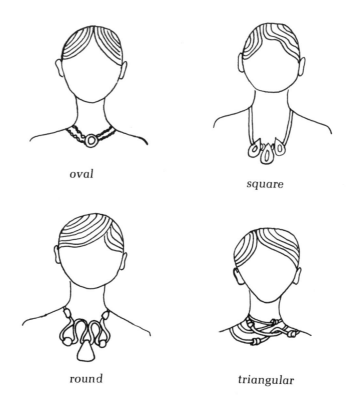

oval

square

round

triangular

WEARER'S COLORING

SKIN, HAIR AND EYE COMBINATION	BEST COLORS
Light pink/brown skin, blonde hair, blue or brown eyes.	Blues and violets.
Light pink/brown skin, light-brown hair, blue or brown eyes.	Blues, greens and some yellows to even out skin tone.
Light pink/brown skin, light-auburn hair, brown eyes.	Greens and blues to intensify hair, deep blues to contrast with hair and warm eyes.
Light yellow/brown skin, medium-brown hair and eyes.	Greens and blues to warm skin.
Light yellow/brown skin, dark-brown hair and eyes.	Greens and blues to warm skin, dark reds and blues to balance light yellow.
Light yellow/brown skin, auburn hair, brown eyes.	Greens and blues to intensify hair. Reds to pick up hair tones and balance yellows in skin.
Medium brown/light-red skin with dark-brown hair and eyes.	Yellows or blues to even skin tones; greens to intensify skin tones, warm hair and eyes.
Medium-brown skin, dark-brown hair, dark-brown eyes.	Any color. Use both light and dark shades for contrast.
Dark medium-brown/red skin, dark hair and eyes.	Blues, greens and violets in light to medium tones.
Dark medium-brown/yellow skin, dark hair and eyes.	Light blues and reds to balance yellow in skin, create contrast.
Dark brown/blue (true black) skin, black hair and eyes.	Medium to pale blues, violets and greens. Bright reds and yellows.

2 · Materials and Equipment

WHEN YOU SEW JEWELRY, you hope to make pieces of lasting quality and value. It makes sense, therefore, to use good materials that will last. You want materials that have a look of luxury.

In choosing the materials for a piece of jewelry, ask yourself the same types of questions you asked in arriving at a design. What is the fabric of the dress with which the piece will be worn? What look do you want the final piece to have? Shiny? Glitzy? Rough? Startling? Your materials should reflect your intentions for the piece.

Materials often directly suggest a jewelry design. The feathered nest pendant in Chapter Four is a good example. I began the project with the skin and feathers of a pheasant, a miracle of natural pattern and color. Two colors that especially pleased me were a deep, iridescent green and a muted copper, both of which I found in the central back feathers of the pheasant.

In the basket where I keep grasses, shells, pine cones and other natural objects, I found some hand-dyed palm fibers. They were the same muted copper color that appeared in the feathers. I twisted some of the palm fibers into twine and coiled them around my fingers.

At that point I decided to make a really elaborate piece, with the palm fibers coiled into free-form basket shapes resembling nests. But when I finished the first step—gluing the feathers onto the leather backing—I realized that the feathers should be the center of attention. The coiled basketry was reduced to a simple, shallow frame.

Many other technical considerations went into the design.

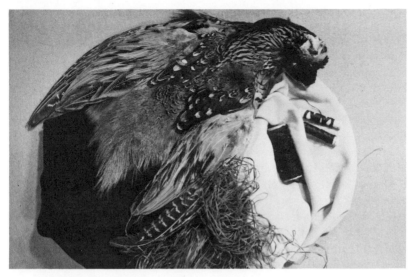

A collection of materials assembled for the feathered nest pendant on page 100. The design took form only after I had handled the materials.

Feathers last longer if they stay flat. So I used fairly thick leather for the base pieces to which the feathers are glued. The small, stuffed shapes were made of very thin lambskin. Its soft texture complements the shiny textures of the feathers and silk thread and the rougher sheen of the palm fibers.

The finished object reflects some common associations of feathers, birds, nests and eggs. But these design ideas were very vague. They only became specific as I worked with the materials.

The more you handle good materials, the more design ideas will come to you. Look for bits of needlework as you shop in antique and import stores. Many of them can be adapted to make jewelry. Look over the clothes your great-aunt left in the attic. The moths may have destroyed the dress, but perhaps the trim can be recycled. Develop the habit of looking for unusual bits of fabric, trim, braid and cord.

The following are some general guidelines for you to follow in the selection of your materials and tools. A specific shopping list is included with each project.

FABRICS

Which fabric you choose for your jewelry depends, first of all, on the technique you will use. For sewing techniques (appliqué, quilting, machine sewing and machine embroidery), the easiest fabrics to use are firmly woven fabrics that do not ravel. If you use other types of fabrics (as I have in some of the projects in this book), you must be prepared for extra work in handling the material.

For batik and tie-dyeing, you will need smooth fabrics without chemical finishes that might impede the action of the dye.

For embroidery, you will need strong fabrics that are loosely woven, so that the needle and thread can slide through easily.

Every fabric has different properties of strength, elasticity, weave and texture. In this book, you will find a strong preference for fabrics made from natural fibers. I think natural fabrics are more pleasing in texture, color and sheen than are synthetic fabrics. Most important, natural fabrics harmonize well with the natural threads—silk, cotton and wool—that are used for fancy sewing and embroidery.

Even if you use only natural fabrics, you still have an immense range from which to choose. Your choice will depend on the technique you use as well as on the visual effects you want to achieve. Other qualities you must consider are the fabric's resistance to dye, colorfastness, ease of handling, ease of maintenance and resistance to wrinkles and stains. Cost and availability are sometimes important factors as well.

No matter where you live in the United States, you can find interesting fabrics with which to work. Your local fabric store and the fabric sections of department stores are the obvious places to begin looking. Remnants counters can be real treasure troves, since small pieces of fabric are very useful for jewelry.

Rummage sales, secondhand clothing stores and garage sales are good places to look for old clothes whose fabrics can be recycled. If you use an old fabric, test it first. Snip a scrap from a facing or hem. Then wash the scrap in soap and water to test its colorfastness, iron it to test its heat-resistance, and tear it to test its strength. Rotting fabric will discolor when ironed and tears very easily.

In many cities, you can buy fabrics at import stores. Mexican import stores sell sturdy, hand-woven cottons; Japanese, Chinese and Indian import stores sell hand-printed cottons, gauzes and silks; African import stores sell block-printed and tie-dyed cottons; and Malaysian import stores sell block-printed and batiked cottons and silks. Import stores also sell little bits of embroidery or other needlework that you can incorporate into your jewelry designs.

The following paragraphs describe the major types of natural fabrics, their qualities and how those qualities will affect your jewelry-making. Space does not permit me to mention every generic or brand name. For more detailed information on a particular fabric, read the label on the bolt.

Silk

Silk is made from the fibers spun by the silkworm (the larva of the moth *Bombyx mori*). The silkworms are fed on mulberry leaves. The larva spins a cocoon around itself. When the cocoon is soaked and heated, the threads can be unwound. One silk fiber might be as much as 100 yards long.

Silk comes in many weights and weaves and is very strong. *Raw silk* has very little sheen and is frequently woven into a nubby-textured cloth. Some raw silk has a loose, open weave that is usable for embroidery. It cannot, however, be used without a backing, since the fabric lacks stiffness.

Silk shantung is woven from thick and thin threads, giving it an uneven texture. Shantungs are tightly woven and are medium to heavy in weight. Their texture keeps them from sliding around as much as other silks do. *China silk* is very shiny and light in weight. *Crepe de Chine* is a lightweight silk that has a soft, pebbly texture. *Silk surah*, another lightweight silk, can be recognized by its diagonal weave.

Often fabrics sold as China silk, crepe de Chine or silk surah are not 100 per cent silk. If you plan to dye the silk, the presence of synthetic fibers might impede the action of the dye. Be sure to read the label.

For most of the jewelry in this book, I used a medium-weight silk called *English silk*. I found that the lightweight silks were too slippery and snagged too often to make them really practical. Lightweight silks are lovely, though, for scarves, head wraps and draped belts.

Unfortunately, most silk is expensive. It can cost $100 a yard— or more. Most silks in fabric stores range from $8 to $25 a yard. The high cost might make silk impractical for use in a collar, cummerbund or other large piece. You might consider using silk for the front of your piece and a less expensive fabric for the back. Old scarves and shawls provide inexpensive silk scraps.

Silk has properties that can make it difficult to handle. Silks are exceptionally clingy—they seem to produce more static electricity than other fabrics. Silk can also slither around when you sew it. To solve both those problems, baste each piece of silk to a backing of thin fabric or tissue paper before you begin to work with it. Sewing and removing basting stitches is boring, and it means spending an extra hour or two on each project. But it will save you hours of frustration, not to mention expensive cloth.

Some silk ravels horribly. It pays to take the extra time to bind the seams. If you're sewing the silk with a tissue-paper layer, you can use the zigzag attachment on your sewing machine to bind the seams. Be sure to use the thinnest available needles for both hand and machine sewing of silk. Otherwise you may have problems with the silk snagging.

Why go to all this trouble with silk? Because no fabric can compare with it for the look and feel of luxury. Silk feels sensuous against the skin. The next time you are at a fabric counter, compare a bolt of pure silk to a bolt of the most expensive synthetic fabric. Your hands and eyes will confirm the difference.

Most silk fabrics absorb dyes very well, making them especially suitable for batik and tie-dyeing. Many silks are unsuitable for embroidery because they are so tightly woven that embroidery needles make holes and runs in them. Heavier, more loosely woven silks make better embroidery ground fabrics. Always use silk thread to embroider on silk.

Some silks can be hand-washed; others must be dry-cleaned. Test a scrap of fabric by washing it in a basin. If the fabric water-spots, it must be dry-cleaned. Colored silk should be prewashed and tested for colorfastness. This is particularly true of silks bought in import stores.

Linen

Linen is made from the fibers of the flax plant. Linen's most desirable qualities are its strength and its beautiful natural sheen. Linen is the best possible ground fabric for embroidery, since its open weave allows needles to slide through easily. Embroideries on linen have lasted for hundreds of years.

Most fabric stores carry only three weights of 100 per cent linen. Most of the pure linen sold in the United States is imported from Ireland. Moygashel is the most widely available brand. Irish linen is expensive, ranging from $9 to $15 a yard.

Heavy linen is best for handbags or other items that will get a lot of use. Medium-weight linen is good for embroidery. Light-weight linen, or *handkerchief linen*, is excellent as a backing for silk. The linen is soft enough to flow with the silk yet strong enough to support it. Subtle see-through effects can be achieved by embroidering on white linen that has been backed with silk in a bright color.

Linens of all weights are sold in their natural colors (dark tan to off-white) and in white. But linen—especially handkerchief linen—dyes well, so many other colors are possible. I think heavy linen looks best in its natural color, which is usually a dark tan.

Linen ravels easily because of its loose weave. Trim the edges with pinking shears to keep them from coming undone as you embroider. For a long-term project, or a project that requires rough handling of the fabric, bind the edges of the linen. You can use the zigzag stitch on your sewing machine for the binding. If you don't bind the edges, ravelling threads will sooner or later knot your embroidery thread.

Linen should be washed, dried and pressed before you begin working with it. Linen wrinkles easily, so you will need to keep ironing it during construction to ensure that your final piece will lie flat.

Cotton

Cotton is made from the fibers of the cotton plant. Cotton fabrics come in many weights, weaves and textures. Cotton's chief virtue for jewelry-making is its availability in a huge range of colors, patterns and finishes. Cotton is the least expensive natural fiber. Although prices are rising all the time, you can still get 100 per cent cotton for as little as $3 a yard.

In its natural state, cotton lacks the lustrousness of linen. However, much commercial cotton has been treated to add such qualities as sheen, colorfastness and resistance to wrinkles and stains. Unfortunately, these finishes inhibit the action of dye. If you tie-dye or batik, you should ask for 100 per cent untreated cotton. *Muslin* is a thin, loosely woven cotton that is often available untreated. Muslin should be washed and preshrunk before use.

Cotton is sold under many generic names. *Batiste, organdy, dimity, lawn* and *voile* are all very lightweight—even sheer—cottons. They are all good for ruffly shawls, scarves and flowing head wraps. They are not suitable for embroidery, since they lack strength. All of these semi-transparent cottons come in lovely floral prints and in white-on-white patterns as well as in plain, usually pastel, colors.

Calico, gingham, muslin, polished cotton and *percale* are all medium to lightweight fabrics that are tightly woven. They can be embroidered with fine thread, but they are at their best when used for quilted and stuffed shapes. The tight weave of these fabrics keeps the edges from ravelling. All these fabrics are easy to handle. They have exciting possibilities for machine appliqué as well as for hand appliqué and patchwork.

The best cottons to use for embroidery are strong, open-weave fabrics such as *drill, bottom-weight gauze, leno, monk's cloth* and *Oxford cloth. Burlap* is also a possibility, but only if a rather rough look is appropriate for your piece.

Many cottons are woven with raised textures. These are called *napped* fabrics. Fabrics with nap are usually unsuitable for batiking, though they can be tie-dyed or painted. Napped fabrics are closely woven, so they are difficult to embroider. Still, napped fabrics—*corduroy, velveteen, flannel, velour* and *terry cloth*—are invaluable when you want a soft, deep texture in a piece.

Special mention should also be made of cottons which are woven with raised patterns, such as *dotted Swiss, waffle cloth, piqué* and *seersucker.* Unusual effects can be achieved by tie-dyeing these fabrics, since the ridges of weaving will absorb the dye unevenly. Embroidering between the raised areas is another good possibility.

Various European countries—France, England, Italy, Sweden and Switzerland—export expensive cottons that are super-luxurious in look, color and feel. For the shell bag in Chapter Seven and the collar in Chapter Five, I used 100 per cent cotton velveteen imported from Italy. The velveteen is much softer and lighter in weight than American velveteen.

Many cottons are medium to heavy weight, tightly woven fabrics that are perfect for bags, belts and other pieces that will get heavy use. *Denim, canvas, duck* and *sailcloth* are among these. Embroidery is difficult on these fabrics, except with a sewing machine. However, all the fabrics are excellent as ground fabrics for machine appliqué. Use the largest (size 16) needle on your sewing machine for working with these fabrics.

Cotton is the easiest natural fiber to care for. Most cottons can be machine washed and dried. Untreated cotton should be prewashed and preshrunk. Almost all cotton made in the United States and Europe has already been preshrunk. Rough-woven cottons from Mexico, India, Pakistan, Bangladesh and South America are usually not preshrunk—in fact, they can shrink up to 20 per cent when washed.

Wool

Wool is made from the fleece of sheep and goats. It comes in a variety of weights and textures. Wool takes hot-water dyeing very well, resulting in soft, subtle shades. Cold-water dyeing, such as is necessary for batik, is less successful. Tie-dyeing with wool can produce brilliant effects of texture and color.

Most wools are considerably more expensive than cottons. However, attractive wool fabrics can still be bought for $5 to $10 a yard. Heavy coat wools can cost $50 to $75 a yard. In between is a wide range of suiting and dress wools. The less expensive "wools" are often blends of wool and synthetic fibers. Read the label for the exact composition of the bolt. Unless you are going to dye the fabric, the presence of synthetic fibers should not hamper your work.

Wools and wool blends are all easy to handle. They have plenty of body and good gripping qualities. They can be kept from ravelling by trimming the edges with pinking shears. Many wools hardly ravel at all.

Smooth, lightweight garment wools are perfect for creating a soft but light texture in a piece. These wools include *wool challis, wool chiffon* and *doeskin*. They are generally not strong enough to use as ground fabrics for embroidery, though they are excellent for quilting and stuffing.

The strongest, most tightly woven wools are the *twill* weaves, which you can recognize by their diagonal lines. Most of these fabrics are too tightly woven for embroidery. But their strength makes them excellent for bags, belts and other heavy-use items. Among the twill weaves are *broadcloth, whipcord, gabardine, serge* and *wool sharkskin*.

Wools with a plain, open weave suitable for embroidery include wool *bunting, homespun* and *hopsacking*.

Heavy coat wools are not suitable for embroidery or appliqué. But they make good fabrics for bags and belts, as well as hats. Coat wools include *tweeds, Mackinaw cloth* and *Melton cloth*.

Felt is a form of wool that deserves special mention. Felt is pressed, not woven. So it has no grain, or direction of weave. Felt can be used for appliquéd shapes that have curved edges. You don't have to hem the edges before you appliqué, since felt will not ravel. I often use felt as a backing, as I did in the stuffed grape pendant in Chapter Four. Before you use felt, though, be sure to wash it to preshrink it and remove extra dye. Then have it dry-cleaned to make it colorfast. Most felt fades and runs.

Many luxury fabrics resemble fine wools, though they are not technically wools since they do not come from sheep or domestic goats. These fabrics include *cashmere, vicuña, llama, alpaca* and *camel's hair.* They are among the most expensive fabrics you can buy. You will find that the more expensive wools are often blended with these fibers.

Wools can be washed in mild laundry soap or dry-cleaned. To preshrink wool, press it several times with a steam iron. As a general rule, the looser the wool's weave, the more likely it will need to be preshrunk.

Perhaps wool's most distinctive quality for the jewelry-maker is that it can be shaped easily with steam. The elegant, perfect fit of a suit from a Paris couture house comes from careful steaming and shaping of each seam and facing. To shape wool, press it over a heavily stuffed form such as a tailor's ham. Press directly down; don't move the iron around on the fabric. Use lots of steam. Then wait until the wool dries before lifting it from the form.

Felt responds especially well to shaping by steam. If you have a tired old felt hat, try steam-pressing it on a tailor's ham and adding a new trim, using some of the ideas you see in this book.

Special Needlework Fabrics

Needlework stores carry special fabrics manufactured especially for various needle crafts. *Belgian linen, Binca cloth, Aida cloth* and *Hardanger cloth* are all strong, open-weave fabrics that are ideal ground fabrics for embroidery. *Irish linen* is also sold in many needlework shops.

For needlepointers, needlework shops carry *needlepoint canvas* in various sizes—10, 12, 13, 14, 16 and 18 squares to the inch are common sizes for single-weave or *mono* canvas. Double-woven canvas, called *Penelope canvas,* has pairs of crossed threads instead of single crossed threads. Penelope sizes are 10/20, 12/24, 14/28, 16/32 or 18/36. *Silk gauze* is tiny, squared-off gauze that is used as the ground for silk petit point.

For counted-thread embroidery, such as cross-stitch, there is *cross-stitch canvas*, which has been one of my favorite fabrics since I was little. Cross-stitch canvas is woven in squares, and the whole cloth is held together with starch. You baste the canvas to your ground fabric, embroider your cross-stitch design in the squares, and then wash the finished piece. The starch disintegrates with moisture, allowing you to pull out the threads of the canvas. Your embroidery, perfectly squared in every stitch, stays on the ground fabric.

Metallic Fabrics

Almost no one can afford real gold or silver fabric any more, so you will have to content yourself with a synthetic imitation. Metallic fabrics look glittering and luxurious. Bits of metallic fabric are perfect for sparkling up an appliquéd or machine-embroidered piece. In general, metallic fabrics are suitable for quilting, sewing and appliqué, but not for embroidery, batik or tie-dyeing.

Lamé is made from nothing but metallic threads. Most lamés are knitted fabrics. The most common colors are gold, silver and copper. Sometimes lamés are also available in deep jewel tones of green, blue and red. Some lamés are quite inexpensive—$5 to $7 a yard—but they look cheap, too. A good lamé should feel heavy to you. It shouldn't feel light and stretchy. You may have to pay up to $15 a yard for good lamé.

When you make a piece of jewelry with lamé, keep the lines simple. The fabric calls enough attention to the piece.

Some fabrics have only a few metallic threads woven in or embroidered on at intervals. I once saw some gorgeous Indian silk chiffon, with multicolored chiffon flowers appliquéd on it. Each flower was outlined in metallic thread. The price: $50 a yard. Some expensive *silk brocades* also have their patterns outlined in this way.

In *sequined fabrics*, tiny circles of metal or plastic are knitted into the cloth.

Many metallic fabrics have dangerously low heat resistance, since the "metals" are really plastic fibers. Be very careful when you iron them. Too high a setting can melt the synthetic fibers quickly, and you may have a fire on your hands. Never press metallic fabric directly; always put a damp cloth between the iron and the fabric.

Some metallic fabrics are difficult to cut and sew. It's a good idea to use paper-cutting scissors, not your best dressmaking shears. You may find that you have to change your sewing machine needle more often when you sew with metallic fabric.

Almost all metallic fabrics should be dry-cleaned. Never put one of these fabrics in a dryer.

LEATHER

In the projects in this book you will be working only with relatively small pieces of leather, used primarily as backing for feathers. You can get small pieces of leather at crafts and hobby shops that will work excellently for these purposes. If you live near a large city, you can also find leather at tanneries and manufacturers of leather goods.

The thinnest leathers can be handled much like fabric. You can even sew them by machine. Care must be taken in sewing, however. Leather is not cloth. Each hole you punch in leather stays there. It is not filled in by the warp and weft threads as it is in cloth. If your stitches in leather are too small, you will make a perforated line that can be easily torn.

On the whole it is easier and more mistake-proof to work small pieces of leather by hand. Use waxed linen thread or silk buttonhole twist for sewing (see section on threads).

One big advantage of leather is that it can be wet, tacked to a contoured form, and dried into a shape. This is the way heavy, shaped leather hats are made. *Cowhide* comes in many thicknesses, from jacket weight to very thick tooling leather. Thinner leathers include *kid, lambskin, chamois, calfskin, deerskin* and *pigskin*. Leather specialty shops sometimes carry various *snakeskins* and *alligator skins*, though conservation laws have made reptiles more rare.

Leather can be surprisingly inexpensive. Scrumptious thin lambskin is about one third the price of high-quality synthetic suede. If you have a tannery in your area (see the Yellow Pages), you will find that you can work with leather for less money than you would spend working with many fabrics.

FUR

Fur is leather from which the hairs have not been removed. For most jewelry projects, you will need only fur scraps. You can get scraps of fur at hobby and crafts shops. If you need larger quantities of fur scraps, look in your Yellow Pages for the names of furriers and manufacturers of fur garments. Weaving supply stores also carry fur at times.

Furs have many different textures. *Persian lamb* is short, wiry and very curly. *Rabbit's fur* and *sheepskin* are both soft furs. They are widely available in the United States. *Mink, beaver, chinchilla* and other luxury furs must be bought by the pelt from furriers. They are extremely expensive.

Many hobby stores and school supply stores sell plastic bags filled with scraps of fur for as little as $3. Most of this fur is rabbit fur, sometimes dyed in various bright colors. *Goat hide* is sometimes also sold in scraps, as is untanned *cowhide.*

When you sew with fur, be careful to sew only its leather backing. If the hairs get caught in the seam the piece will look messy.

Spreading hairs are another sewing problem. Cover the feed area of your machine when you sew with fur. Tissue paper or construction paper will protect the bobbin case while you sew.

Small bits of fur can be glued onto leather or even cloth. Elmer's or a similar white glue is fine for this job. For larger sewing jobs, you can use either a sewing machine or a large leather needle and waxed linen thread. Which technique you use depends on the thickness of the leather to which the fur is attached. In general, it is a good idea to keep fur designs very simple. The pattern and texture of the fur already provide enough detail.

INTERFACING AND STUFFING

Many of the projects in this book are worked in layers. The outer layers are embroidered or otherwise decorated. But the inner layers—those that add stiffness and strength to the pieces—are just as important. Synthetic fabrics do have their place, and their qualities work very well for interfacing and stuffing.

Nonwoven polyester interfacing is sold at fabric counters and is available in light, medium and heavy weights. Pellon is the most common brand. Use heavy interfacing for handbags, pendants, belts and stiff collars. Use medium-weight interfacing for backing cotton and linen in softer collars and pendants. Silk should be backed only with lightweight interfacing, unless there is another backing in between. For the couched and coiled silk pendant in Chapter Four, for example, I first attached the silk to medium-weight linen and then to heavy interfacing. Had I attached the silk directly to the interfacing, the difference in weights would have caused the silk to sag.

Cotton batting and stuffing are still available through Wards, Sears and other mail-order catalogs and in some conservative department stores. But the cotton products are rapidly being replaced by the polyester.

Polyester batting and stuffing have many advantages over their cotton counterparts. Super-fluff is a widely available brand. The synthetics are lighter and fluffier. They do not wad up when they are washed, as do the cotton products. Batting comes pressed into large, thin sheets. Use batting for large pieces that must be uniform in thickness, such as the appliquéd cummerbund on page 139. Use stuffing, which is sold loose and formless, for filling small shapes like beads.

METAL JEWELRY FINDINGS

In this book I have tried to avoid using any metal, even for closures. But sometimes that rule can't be followed, as in the case of earrings. Crafts and hobby stores sell small metal jewelry findings—ear clips for nonpierced ears, ear backs, posts and wire for pierced ears, and backs for hairpins, brooches and pins. The whip stitch (see Index of Techniques) is useful for attaching soft beads and other forms to the findings.

THREADS

Threads are made from many types of natural and synthetic fibers. In this section, I will describe only the threads that are needed for the various soft jewelry projects in this book. Most of these threads are sold at art needlework counters and needlepoint shops. They are manufactured especially for use in embroidery and other fancy needlework.

The easiest threads with which to work are firm, medium weight, and fairly uniform in thickness. If your thread is too soft, you will have trouble shaping your stitches. If it is too stiff, you will find it difficult to make even stitches or to keep them in place.

It pays to take the time to select the right thread for your project. In general, your thread should be of the same fiber as your background fabric. Some exceptions are noted in the paragraphs that follow.

Machine sewing threads are sold in spools and come in a huge variety of colors. They can be used for hems and other hand sewing as well as for machine embroidery. Belding Corticelli, J.P. Coats, Talon and Fruit of the Loom are widely available brands.

Belding Corticelli makes 100 percent cotton threads in various weights. Weights of cotton thread are indicated by numbers. The smaller the number, the finer the thread. Number 50 is the medium weight sold for general machine and hand sewing. I like Belding Corticelli's threads because their colors seem less harsh and synthetic.

J.P. Coats manufactures Double Duty thread, which has a core of polyester and a covering of cotton. This thread is billed as being usable on all types of fabrics. To tell the truth, silk machine sewing thread is still preferable for silk, and cotton still works best on cotton.

Silk sewing-machine thread is not always available except at better department stores and needlework shops. D.M.C. and Belding Corticelli are two well-known brands. Silk threads are graded by letter, with A being the finest thread and D being the thickness of silk buttonhole twist. A Spanish company, La Paleta, has begun distributing their silk buttonhole twist in crafts stores in the United States. La Paleta threads are wound on thin cardboard spools and come in an incredible variety of subtle colors.

Several firms manufacture special threads for *machine embroidery*. Belding Corticelli and D.M.C. are two such firms. Zwicky machine-embroidery thread, another excellent brand, is also available at some needlework shops. All of these threads give better results than ordinary thread for machine appliqué, machine embroidery and machine quilting.

Hand embroidery threads are available at variety stores, department store needlework counters, and needlework shops. Silk embroidery thread has a lovely sheen and a rich texture. D.M.C., Zwicky and Pearsall are all excellent brand names. You can sometimes also get silk embroidery thread at Indian and Pakistani stores, though these threads are sometimes too soft and slippery to work with easily. Silk buttonhole twist can also be used effectively in embroidery; in fact, most of the embroidery in this book was done with La Paleta's buttonhole twist. Buttonhole twist, as the name implies, is a twisted thread. Regular silk embroidery thread is less tightly twisted, or plied. The difference is in texture. Buttonhole twist will be less shiny than regular silk embroidery thread.

Cotton embroidery floss is an excellent all-around material for jewelry. The six-strand threads will keep their shape when crocheted, braided or knitted. They are textured enough to hold knots firmly. They are easy to handle, very inexpensive and available nearly everywhere. Coats and Clark embroidery floss is available at Woolworth's and other variety stores. D.M.C. floss is carried by department stores and needlework shops. D.M.C. threads come in subtle, less chemical-looking colors than do Coats and Clark threads.

Crewel wools are thin wool yarns that are used for embroidery on linen or wool. Crewels come in lovely shades—every conceivable color is available. D.M.C., Elsa Williams, Appleton, Paternayan and Orchidee are some brand names. Because wool dyes so richly, crewel colors are softer, richer and more subtle than silk or cotton colors. The texture of crewel shows off expert stitchery to perfection. Crewel wools can be used on linens, open-weave cottons such as Hardanger cloth, or on open-weave wools.

Crochet threads are available at variety stores and needlework shops in fine and medium weights. I have found that many variety stores carry only a few colors, usually pastels and black and white. Larger department stores and needlework shops have a wider range of colors. Some cotton crochet threads are variegated, so that their shade or colors change as you work with them. You can make your own stunning, irregularly variegated thread by tie-dyeing plain white cotton thread.

Threads for macramé include cotton string and cord, jute, thin rope and linen string or cord. These are all available at hardware stores in their natural shades or at macramé supply stores in bright colors. Plastic twine, fish line, and baling twine are other good possibilities. All are available at hardware stores.

Waxed linen thread is a good all-around thread for heavy-use projects such as bags and belts. Waxed linen thread is intended for sewing leather, but it has a multitude of uses in braiding, crochet, macramé and wrapping. You will see it used in several of the projects in this book.

YARNS

Yarns come in a variety of weights and textures and are spun from many different fibers. No matter what their fiber content, yarns can be classified according to the technique used in spinning them. *Unplied* or untwisted yarns are very loosely spun. Many yarns used in handweaving are unplied. *Plied yarns* consist of various unplied yarns twisted together. Two-ply yarns are twisted from two yarns; 4-ply yarns are twisted from four strands, and so forth. The more tightly plied a yarn is, the stronger and stiffer it will be.

Yarns are suitable for crochet, knitting, braiding, wrapping and, sometimes, macramé. The smoother and more tightly plied a yarn is, the easier it will be to work with. But the smoother the yarn, the more regular will be the texture of your finished piece. If you want to use thick, fuzzy yarns, you must be prepared for some extra catching and snagging as you work.

Yarns that are too thick to pass through a ground fabric can still be incorporated into an embroidered piece. *Couching* (see page 108) is an embroidery technique used to attach thick threads, cords or yarns to the surface of fabrics.

In general, handspun yarns are more desirable than machine-spun yarns. Handspun yarn has interesting variations of texture; machine-spun yarns are too flat and regular. Best of all are the yarns that are handspun and hand-dyed in natural dyes. The resulting colors are as luscious and subtle as the textures. Handspun yarns are available at weaving supply stores and some needlecraft shops. They can also be ordered from yarn suppliers. Some addresses of yarn suppliers are listed in the back of this book.

Some machine-spun wools are spun unevenly or dyed unevenly to give them extra interest. Novelty wools such as bouclés and chenilles are among these. The most beautiful machine-spun wools, I think, are those that combine wool with other fibers such as metallic threads, alpaca fibers or silk thread.

Wool yarns are spun from the fleece of sheep. They vary greatly in texture and thickness. Beautiful, thick wools can be up to an inch thick. Wools are sold in their natural colors—whites, browns, grays and blacks—as well as in dyed colors. Wool yarns take dye very well, so you might want to order white or off-white wool in larger quantities and dye small quantities yourself. Most wool suppliers will provide information on the dyeing qualities of their various yarns.

Wool can also be bought in its unspun state. Spinning yarn yourself can open up a whole new world of textural possibilities, since you can vary the width of the yarn according to your own exact specifications.

Some natural wools and wool yarns come to you feeling a bit greasy and with little bits of grass spun in. If you want to remove this rough texture (for jewelry that will be worn next to the skin), you should wash the wool or yarn in mild laundry detergent and, perhaps, fabric softener. Wash the finished item as well.

Linen yarns are exceptionally strong. Slubbed linen and other unevenly spun linens are much stronger than similarly spun wools—a good thing to keep in mind when you want both strength and a nubby texture. Linen yarns also have more stiffness than wool. Even very soft linen yarns are so strong that you can pull knots and loops very tight, giving stiffness to the final piece.

Linen yarns are less widely available than wools. There are fewer varieties of linen available as well. However, linen yarns can be ordered from certain yarn suppliers. They are also sometimes carried by weaving supply stores.

Linen threads have a lovely shell-like polish, which is maintained over repeated washings. They dye very well, in clear, bright colors.

Synthetic yarns come in a wide variety of textures. The standard knitting yarns are, like their wool counterparts, too soft and uninteresting for jewelry. Another problem is that most synthetic yarns stretch as you handle them. The best synthetic threads for jewelry are the novelty spins such as lamé and other metallic threads. Lamé threads are especially well suited to jewelry, not only because of their glow but because of their strength. Lamé threads sometimes split if they are not handled carefully, but they are quite easy to work with after a little practice. Most synthetic yarns take dye all too well—the results are undesirably electric.

FEATHERS

The chief requirement for a feather design is that it be kept simple, because feathers are not easy to handle. Each feather's stem sprouts thousands of little pieces of fluff, which come off and get into your sewing machine and your sinuses.

Many problems can be avoided by using feathers that are sold threaded on a long string. If you have a whole skin, pluck each feather individually, attach it, and then pluck the next one. The fluff will spread anyway, but care helps keep it down.

If you are sewing over feathers with a sewing machine, put some layers of tissue paper between the pressure foot and the feeder to keep the fluff from damaging the machine works.

Feathers are available at crafts supply stores and at an increasing number of notions counters. You can also buy dyed feathers at variety and discount stores, but such feathers I would never use in jewelry. Feathers in their natural patterns are far more spectacular.

TRIMS, LACES, CORDS AND RIBBONS

In the past an enormous profusion of braids and trims was available in fabric stores. The beaded braids, trims, cords and buttons of the Victorian, Edwardian and Jazz eras can still be found in antique shops, secondhand clothing stores and attics. These remain your best sources for really unusual bits of trim. In some big cities, there are shops specializing in trims. Such shops offer a much wider selection than is generally available.

But for many consumers, the choices are more limited. A fabric store may carry hundreds of trims, but few of them will have

A collection of cords and ribbons, many of which were used for projects in this book. The white silky cord on the large spool and the rougher white cords in front were dyed to go with various designs. (Cords and ribbons from Vogue Fabrics, Evanston, Illinois, and Tinsel Trading Company, New York.)

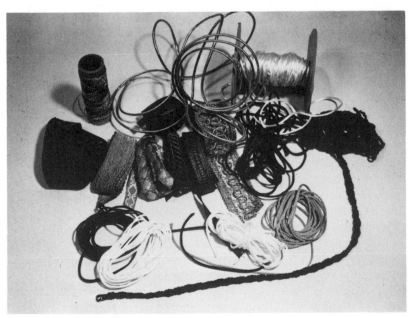

anything but the look of the machine. Another problem is the almost universal use of synthetics for trims. You should never use any trim without testing it for colorfastness, shrinking, puckering and heat resistance. I've had too many disasters with cheaply made ribbons that bled all over my embroidery or with lace that unravelled when I pulled the wrong thread. It is better to buy six inches of trim and test it than to waste your money on an inferior product.

Real *silk cord* is nearly impossible to find in most communities in the United States. Unless you live in New York City, you will almost certainly have to settle for a cheap-looking synthetic product. In Chapter Three, "Cords, Trims, Beads and Closures," you will learn how to make your own bias cord as well as how to make commercial cords look more appealing.

Ribbons have suffered a similar fate. Take your time and look for really nice ribbons, even though they cost more. Find ribbons that are tightly woven and that have interesting designs and subtle colors. Once you start sewing jewelry, you will want to start collecting odd bits of trim from old garments.

Many *drapery cords* have a formal, polished appearance that suits jewelry far better than does the sleazy finish of synthetic ribbons. When you are shopping for cords, be sure to check the drapery and upholstery sections of your local department stores. Cotton drapery cording comes in many thicknesses and can be covered with bias fabric to make original-looking cord. Upholstery departments also sell frog fasteners, buttons, large fabric beads and tassels, all of which suggest possibilities to the maker of needle-made jewelry.

TOOLS AND EQUIPMENT

The tools for sewing jewelry can be bought at any dime store for very little money. Talon, Singer, J.P. Coats and Dritz are the most widely distributed brands of sewing and embroidery tools. But care must be taken in choosing them. Using the wrong tool can ruin a project.

Sewing-machine needles vary in size, from 9 for lightweight fabrics to 16 for heavy fabrics. You can buy packages with assorted sizes. It is important to use the right needle size for the fabric, to prevent snagging or irregular tension.

Hand-sewing needles should also be of the proper size for the fabric you are using. The only real way to determine the right size

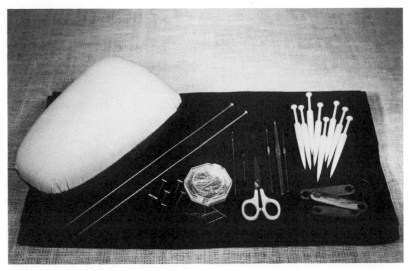

Some tools for sewing jewelry include (left to right) a tailor's ham, knitting needles, T-pins, dressmaker's pins, tapestry and embroidery needles, embroidery scissors, crochet hooks, bobbins and shuttles. The tools are displayed on a soft workboard.

is to slide the needle through the fabric. Fortunately, you can buy assorted needles in packages that will guarantee you will have the right size. You will also need a needle with an eye large enough for the thread you are using to pass through. Experiment to find the best combination of needle, fabric and thread.

Crewel needles have large eyes shaped like slits. These eyes make it easier to thread embroidery floss through them. I used crewel needles for all the embroidery in this book. Crewels come in numbered sizes—the higher the number, the smaller the needle. For embroidering on medium-weight silk backed with handkerchief linen, I used silk buttonhole twist and a number 7 crewel needle.

Tapestry needles have large eyes and blunt points. They are used for making lace, sewing prepunched leather, and other sewing processes that don't require punching through fabric. Tapestry needles, which are often called *crafts needles*, can be found at your dime store. Many dime stores also sell handy little sets of hobby needles. A set might include tapestry, sailmaking, and curved and straight leatherwork needles.

Pins come in many thicknesses. Only the thinnest ones you can find should be used for silk. Larger *dressmaker's pins* can be used for linen and cotton. For anchoring lace and leatherwork, you will need large *T-pins,* also called *macramé pins.*

Scissors should be kept as sharp as possible. A small pair of *embroidery scissors* is invaluable for close work. If you attempt to use larger scissors to clip a seam, for example, your hand could easily slip and slash the fabric. You will need larger scissors, of course, for cutting fabric, as well as a duller pair of scissors for cutting paper patterns, leather, feathers and cord. Never use fabric scissors for anything but fabric. Your scissors should be the best ones you can afford, especially if you do a lot of sewing.

Embroidery hoops hold your jewelry in place as you work. Hoops come in many sizes. The size indicates the diameter of the hoop in inches. They are made of wood, metal or plastic. I prefer the soft plastic hoops, as they seem to hold the fabric tighter. If you do batik, by the way, you will find an embroidery frame is all you need for small pieces.

A *soft workboard* and a *tailor's ham* frequently come in handy in making jewelry. Both are firm but soft work surfaces. You push pins directly into the surface to hold your work in place. A tailor's ham can be bought at any sewing notions counter. Soft workboards, such as macramé boards, can be bought at hobby shops. But it is just as easy to make a soft workboard yourself. Just glue three or four pieces of corrugated cardboard together and press them dry. Wrap a few layers of polyester batting around the cardboard and then a few layers of old fabric around the batting. Staple or pin the construction in place.

Crochet hooks are useful for many jobs besides crochet. The blunt end of a large crochet hook is the perfect tool for stuffing beads. Very fine crochet hooks are useful for tying knots in short threads. Crochet hooks come in both numbered and lettered sizes. Sizes 000 to 10 and above are fine hooks. As with needles, the higher the number, the smaller the hook. Larger hooks are numbered alphabetically, with A being the smallest hook. You can buy sets of assorted sizes, but crochet hooks are also sold individually.

Knitting needles are made from metal or plastic and are sized by number. The larger the number, the larger the needle. A size 20 needle is about an inch in diameter and is suitable for making knitted rugs.

Small *shuttles* and *bobbins* are useful for keeping your work untangled during braiding and twisting. They also speed up the work of macramé.

Clamp clothespins have a thousand uses in jewelry making. They can be used to hold feathers in place while glue is drying, to anchor rolled ribbon beads while they dry, to lift small fabric swatches out of boiling hot dye, and to help hold work in place on a soft workboard or in a frame.

An *iron* and *ironing board* are as indispensable to sewing jewelry as they are to sewing clothing. Pressing your work during its construction helps it keep its shape and helps you keep the work smooth. If you are short of space, a small sleeve ironing board, available at notions counters, is a great convenience.

Tracing paper and *dressmaker's carbon* are needed for transferring designs from this book to your cloth. All the designs are actual size.

3 · Cords, Trims, Beads and Closures

A BEAD OR SERIES OF BEADS strung on a cord or chain and worn around the neck is the most basic form of jewelry. Beads on cords can be braided, wrapped around waists, wrists, and ankles, or coiled and knotted in the hair. Even when another part of the jewelry—such as a pendant or bag—is the main center of attention in a piece of jewelry, cords and beads provide important finishing touches. Details such as hand-embroidered beads can make your work distinctive and elegant.

This chapter will show you how to make a variety of cords, how to achieve decorative effects with trims, how to make several basic beads and how to make professional-looking closures. You can combine cords, trims, and beads in an infinite number of ways. At the end of this chapter, there are step-by-step instructions for making four pieces of soft jewelry, all of which depend on cords and beads.

All too often the selection of cords and trims at your fabric store is very poor, limited to fringes, pompons, and synthetic ribbons and laces. Such cords detract from the value of your sewn jewelry. Here are some ways you can work with ordinary cords and trims to make them special. A handmade cord can also be a piece of jewelry all by itself.

BRAIDING

You probably learned your first braid in the Girl Scouts or when you made lanyards in summer camp. In braiding, the cords form

Stuffed beads of blue silk are embroidered in light-gray silk buttonhole twist and strung on a knotted black cord.

patterns that give the finished rope an interesting texture. You can achieve some really spectacular effects by tie-dyeing smooth synthetic cord and then braiding it.

The easiest cords to braid are perfectly round, smooth, firm and slightly stiff. Softer yarns still work, but extra care must be taken

The four-cord braid.

in handling them. The most unusual braids are made with several different yarns, in subtle combinations of color and texture.

In the picture, the cords are being arranged in a *four-cord braid*. The pattern of the braid is under two and back over one, first from the left and then from the right. For easy mobility anchor the cord by wrapping it around a heavier object, like a clothespin or a wooden ice cream spoon. After each pass of the cord, straighten all four cords, pulling gently but firmly until the braid is as tight as you want. If you lose track of where you are, remember that the top thread always goes next.

WRAPPING

Wrapping serves both to decorate threads and to attach them to other threads. Wrapping is also used to hold loose ends in place, to attach feathers or other objects to cords, to stiffen and strengthen threads, and to create patterns and textures. A beautiful example of wrapping can be found in the Moroccan headdress on page 59.

Wrapping is easiest if you do only a small section at a time. The wrapping thread should be 12 to 15 inches long. Fold over about 3 inches at one end of the wrapping thread. Lay the loop next to the base cords—the cords to be wrapped. Position the loop so that its "tail" lies below the area you want to wrap.

Grasp the base cords and the loop of the wrapping thread at the point you want the wrapping to begin. With your other hand, wrap the long end of the thread around both the loop and the base cords. Be sure to leave the tail of the loop hanging out. Keep your fingers pinched until the loop is being firmly held in place by the wrapping thread.

Keep wrapping until the section is as wide as you want it or until you are close to the loop. On each wrap, lay the thread as close as possible to its previous coil, so that little or no base cord shows. When you finish the wrapped section, thread the end of the wrapping thread through the loop. If you are working with

The sheen of silk adds luxury to an ordinary costume. The silk scarf came from Turkey. The wrapped silk headband came from Morocco. The stuffed silk necklace comes from your own fingers. (Photographed at Just Whistle, Chicago.)

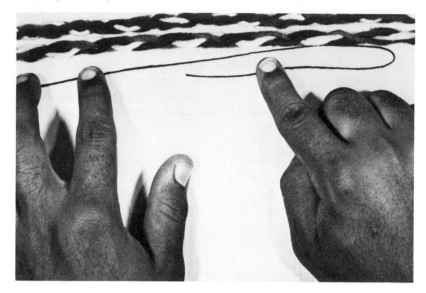

Wrapping: the starting loop.

Beginning to wrap.

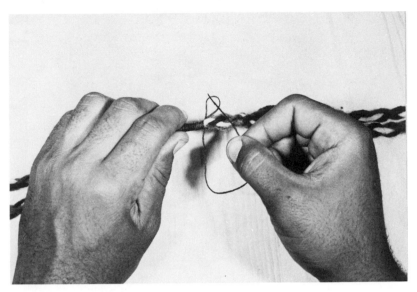

Threading the ends of the wrapping thread through the loop.

Pulling the threads tight.

Braided and wrapped belt in handspun wool, wrapped with waxed linen and silver threads. The braided ends pass through both loops and then back through one loop to fasten the belt.

Wrapping is especially useful in attaching feathers to the ends of cords. Wrap the feather stems and the cords together.

super-fine thread, use a needle to thread the wrapping thread through the loop.

Pull the two ends in opposite directions, away from the wrapping, until the loop slides under the wrapping. Pull slowly so that the wrapping thread will move smoothly without fraying. Clip the ends close to the wrapping.

CROCHETING

The chain stitch, the basic stitch of crochet, can also be used to give texture to cords. Start the chain by tying a loop in one end of the thread or cord. Then use the hook to pull another loop through the first one. Keep pulling loops through each other to make the chain. To end the chain, snip off the cord and pull it all the way through the loop into a knot.

Crocheting in a chain stitch.

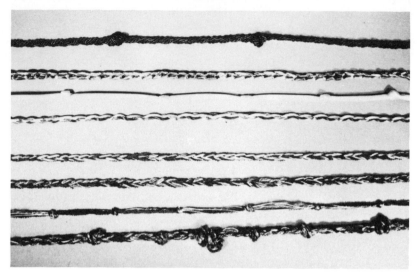

Cords can be braided, knotted and crocheted for a variety of styles and textures.

ORNAMENTAL KNOTTING

Fancy knots can be used both as fasteners and as decorative elements. Even the simplest knots add texture to a plain cord. The diagram shows two knots, the simple overhand knot and the butterfly knot, worked in polyester cord. After you master these, you will want to learn other, more complex, knots.

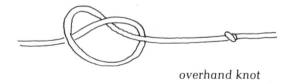

overhand knot

Two simple knots, the overhand and the butterfly, produce different textures in a cord.

butterfly knot

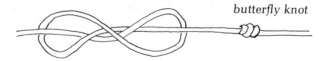

Butterfly Sachet Pendant

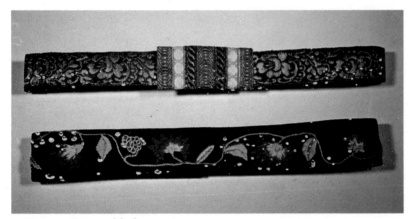

Ribbon and crewel belts

Coiled Snake Pendant

Butterfly Pendant

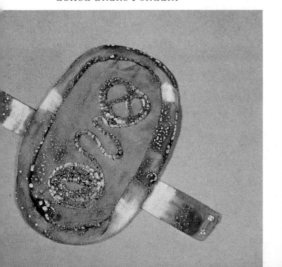

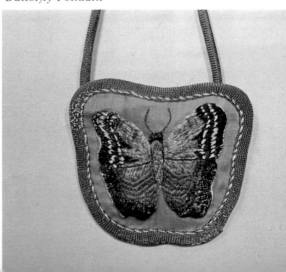

Quilted Butterfly Envelope Purse

Necklace of stuffed silk bias tape with barrel beads

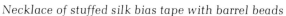

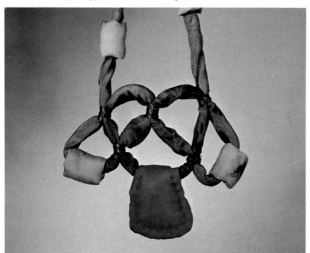

Feathers wrapped onto
silk cord

Quilted grape cummerbund

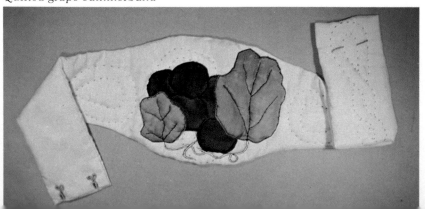

Bias tape bracelets

Tab beads on woven
bias cord

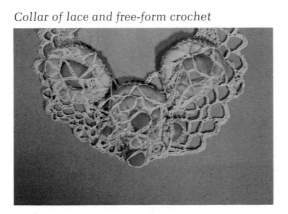

Small silk bags on
drawstring cord

Collar of lace and free-form crochet

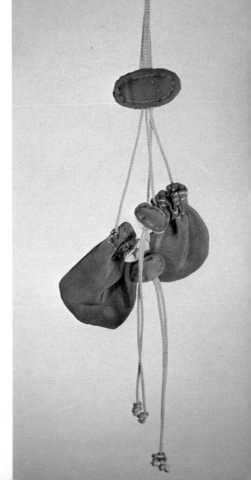

Stuffed Grape Pendant

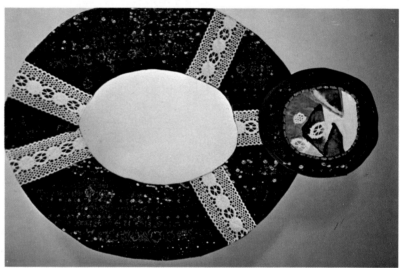

Victorian Round Collar, with Mountain Landscape Pendant attached

Stuffed barrel beads
on silk cord

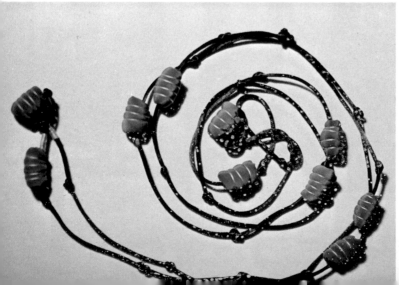

WORKING WITH BIAS TAPE

Bias tape is made from fabric that is cut on the diagonal, across the grain, or weave, of the fabric. Bias tape is available at fabric counters in a wide range of colors but not in a wide range of fabrics, textures or widths. Most commercial bias tape is cotton or polyester, plain woven. It comes in two widths. Single-fold bias tape has the edges pressed under on both sides. Double-fold bias tape is folded once more in the middle. Most bias tape is one-half inch wide, though some stores carry one-inch tape as well. Coats and Clark and Wright's both make fancy bias tapes from cotton prints.

Some bias tapes are made by weaving the finished tape rather than by cutting it from fabric. Many fabric departments carry a woven synthetic bias tape that has a shiny, silky texture. You will find that tape used in many of the projects in this book (see pages 85 and 89).

Because it is cut on the diagonal, bias tape will stretch around curves. You will find it very useful in sewing jewelry. Edges bound with bias tape will lie flat against the curves of your body; cords made with bias tape will be flexible and move when you do.

Making Your Own Bias Tape

Since bias tape comes in such a limited range of fabrics and textures, you may have to make your own. Silk bias tape, for example, is almost impossible to find. You can make bias tape from any woven fabric, from heavy wool tweeds to the lightest chiffons.

Begin with a square of fabric. The square in this example is medium-weight silk that has been tie-dyed in white, gold and dark brown. As always when you work with silk, you must begin by basting the fabric to a piece of tissue paper. If you are working with heavier fabric that does not slide, you can skip this step. Machine-baste diagonal lines across your fabric square, using your machine's longest stitch. Then machine-baste other lines parallel to this central diagonal. The width between the lines should be a little less than twice the width you want your finished tape to be. Stitch another line right next to each diagonal line. You will cut the tape between these narrow pairs of lines, leaving machine sewing along the edges of the diagonal strips.

Your next step will be to sew the diagonal strips together into one long tape. To sew the strips, place the right sides together

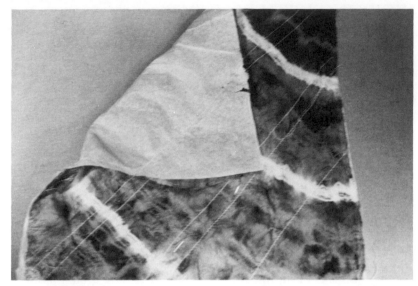

A square of silk, machine-basted on the diagonal (bias) of the fabric. The strips will make bias tape. To dye a square in this pattern, fold the cloth as you would a paper airplane. Wrap rubber bands around at regular intervals. Dip the cloth in gold dye and rinse. Next wrap the areas you want to remain gold and dye the cloth brown. The finished cloth will have a circular stripe.

Connecting strips of bias tape.

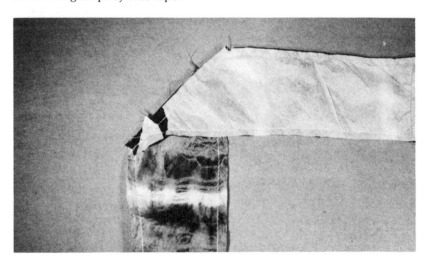

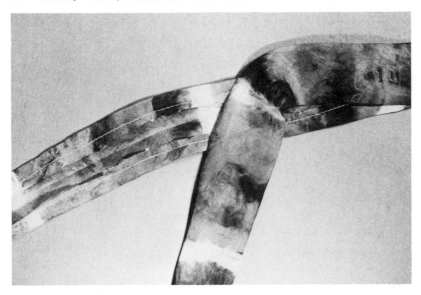

The finished tape, pressed and ready to use. This tape could be bound over a silk cord, as it was for the necklace on page 79, or used to bind an edge, as it was in the coiled snake pendant in Chapter Four.

and arrange the diagonal ends so that the two strips are at right angles. If you are making tape from a slippery fabric, keep the tissue paper on until the strips are sewn together.

Keep adding diagonal strips until your tape is as long as you want it. Then tear the tissue paper off. Fold under both edges of the tape and press the folds. The tape is now ready to use.

Sewing Bias Tape over Cord

Cotton drapery cord, which is available in many fabric departments, makes an excellent core for bias tape. Just lay the drapery cord in the center of the tape and stitch the edges of the tape together over the cord, using a hem stitch (see Index of Tech-

Hem stitch, also called whip stitch or overhand stitch.

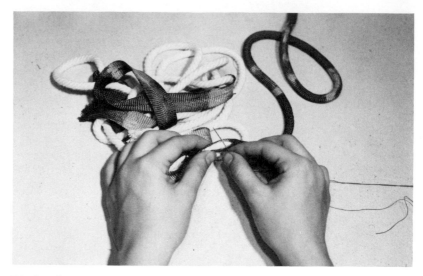

Binding bias tape over cord.

niques). If you like you can tie-dye the bias tape before sewing it over the cord.

Bias-covered cord is used to hang many of the pieces in this book. The cord being made in this picture is used for the necklace on page 85.

DECORATING RIBBONS AND TAPES WITH EMBROIDERY

Simple decorative embroidery can be used to make commercial ribbons and bias tapes more exciting. Such embroidery also saves time, since you attach the ribbon or bias tape with stitches that will be seen.

All the fancy tapes on this sampler were made either from cotton bias tape or from common grosgrain ribbon. They were attached to the ground fabric with running stitches in 6-strand cotton embroidery floss. More thread was looped through the stitches on the surface of the fabric.

The running stitch is the simple in-and-out stitch you learned in kindergarten, the one stitch everyone seems to know how to sew. You might like to work a sampler like this one. Or make

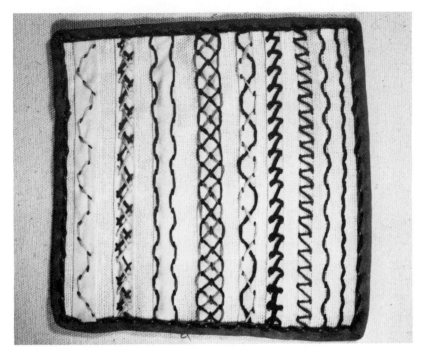

Decorative embroidery on commercial trims—a sampler.

rows of running stitches right on your cloth and experiment with making loops between them. Throughout this book you will see decorated running stitches used to attach trims and linings. This is one of the most useful techniques I know for sewing jewelry.

The simple running stitch. This stitch is also used for quilting.

The decorated running stitch.

A double row of running stitches decorated at random.

SOFT BEADS

Soft beads can be created from any fabric and in any shape. They can be made even more detailed by using tie-dyed fabric or by adding decorative embroidery. Here are instructions for making five kinds of beads. I hope these instructions will give you ideas for other forms. The possibilities are endless.

Tab Beads

Tab beads are elongated in shape. They hang from their narrow ends. The tab on each bead is folded over to form a loop through which the cord can be threaded. Tab beads can be made in any size or shape. Leaf shapes are especially nice.

MATERIALS (for each bead):
    Scrap of silk, at least 3 by 4 inches
    Scrap of linen, the same size
    Sewing thread
    Polyester fiber stuffing
    Silk buttonhole twist (for quilting)

The evolution of a tab bead. The step on the right shows both the front and back of the bead.

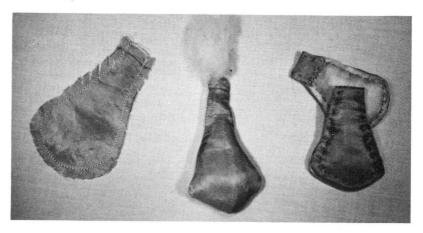

TOOLS:
Sewing needle (size 10, 11, or 12)
Sewing machine

Choose the scraps of silk for your bead. If you are making a large number of beads, you may want to sew several at the same time and then cut them apart later. Trace one of the patterns from this page. Use carbon paper to transfer the pattern to a scrap of cloth.

Patterns for making three kinds of tab beads.

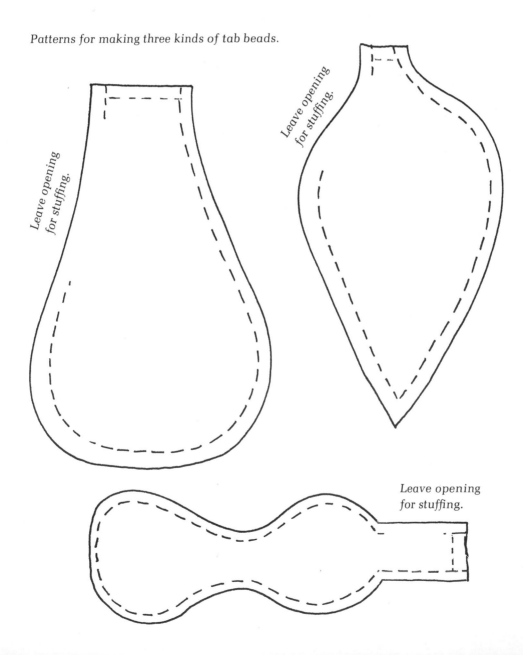

Leave opening for stuffing.

Leave opening for stuffing.

Leave opening for stuffing.

Cut two shapes for each bead, a silk shape for the front of the bead and a linen shape for the back. On these patterns, I have included a seam allowance of about ⅓ of an inch. The inner broken line is the sewing line. If you are working with exceptionally slippery silk, or if you are a novice seamstress, you may want to use a larger seam allowance. In that case, cut about ¼ inch out from the edge of this pattern.

Using a sewing machine, carefully sew the front and the back of the bead together. If your silk has a right and wrong side, the right side should face in. Leave an opening along the neck of the bead, through which to turn the bead inside out. It is very difficult to turn the bead through the narrow neck opening.

After sewing the seam, clip carefully all around the outer edge. Each clip should come in only as far as the sewing line. Be careful not to cut through the seam. The clips help the cloth spread out, so that when you turn the bead inside out the curves will be smooth. The drawing on page 95 shows you how to clip curved edges.

Turn the bead inside out. Use the eraser end of a pencil or the blunt end of a crochet hook to help you with the turning if the opening is too small for your fingers to handle. Then stuff the bead with polyester fiber stuffing and sew the opening closed with slip stitches (see Index of Techniques).

On this bead, I also added a row of quilting about 1 cm (⅓ inch) in from the edge. The photograph shows what both the front and back of the bead look like.

Turn over the tab end so that it forms a loop. Sew the loop down with whip (overcast) stitches (see Index of Techniques).

SUGGESTED VARIATIONS:
Tab beads can be made in any shape. Some suggested shapes are shown in the drawing.

A tab bead can form the base for a really large, elaborate bead. You might also want to try dangling things from a tab bead—cords, threads, feathers or even tiny cloth beads.

Tab beads lend themselves naturally to any long, thin shape. The patterns shown here can be used to make a variety of beads.

Crocheted Round Beads

MATERIALS: TOOLS:
   Yarn or thread   Crochet hook
   Polyester fiber stuffing

To start a bead, crochet a chain of six stitches using the chain stitch as explained on page 63. Use a slip stitch to make the chain into a ring. To make a slip stitch, poke your hook through the first loop you made. There should now be two loops on your hook. Now, pull the thread through both loops.

Make one stitch up from the loop. Then dip your hook through the ring and pull a loop of thread through. Again you should have two loops on your hook. Pull the thread through both these loops. You have just made a single crochet stitch.

Make eleven more single crochet stitches in the center of the ring. At the end, slip stitch the circle closed. Make another stitch up from the loop. Go around the circle again, this time making two single crochets in each loop in the first row. Slip stitch the circle closed.

Go around the circle a third time. This time make only one stitch in each stitch below. Your circle will begin to curve up in a cup shape.

Continue crocheting around, one stitch per loop. If you are like most people, you will soon lose track of the beginnings of the rows. Don't worry about it; just crochet in a spiral until your bead is almost as large as you want it. Your only problem will be counting rows so that a set of beads will be of uniform size. An

Crocheting a bead into a cup shape.

Stuffing a crocheted bead.

easy solution is to count stitches instead, beginning with the first stitch on your chain.

When the bead is almost as large as you want it, begin skipping every third stitch. This will decrease the number of stitches in each row, and your bead will begin to round off. Go around once this way. Then start skipping every other stitch. If you are going to stuff your bead, do it at this point. Keep going around, skipping stitches and decreasing the bead, until you have only one stitch left.

Snip the thread and pull it through the loop. Then use your hook to pull both the beginning and ending threads inside your bead. Your bead is now ready to string.

SUGGESTED VARIATIONS:

Crochet tiny "pearl" beads using very fine crochet linen or cotton and a small (00, 0 or 1) crochet hook. These beads do not have to be stuffed. Make long strings of pearls in white or in pastel colors. Shell colors would be especially lovely.

Crochet several tiny beads in purple crochet cotton. Sew them together to make a small bunch of grapes that could be dangled from an earring or sewed to a pendant.

Choose five or six yarns in varying colors and textures. For a necklace in autumn colors, you might choose crewel wools in oranges and browns, silks in reds and red-oranges, handspun wool in yellows, browns and oranges, waxed linen thread in dark brown, and nubby linen in yellow-green. Crochet beads of different sizes and materials and string them in an interesting pattern.

Crocheted Jewelled Beads

To start this bead, make a short crocheted chain. Then work single crochet stitches back along the chain. Work three single crochets in the original loop, to aid you in turning the corner. Single crochet back along the other side of the chain. Go around in this fashion, making three stitches to turn corners, until the rectangular shape is the size you want it.

Next, start crocheting up from this flat surface. With slip stitches, crochet a circle on the top surface of the crocheted base. Then use those slip stitches for the first row of setting to be crocheted from the base. You will soon be crocheting in a ring, just as you did in making a round bead.

When your setting is as deep as you want it, snip off the thread, knot it, and pull it to the back of the bead.

To make the jewel, cut a small silk circle and gather it around the edge with running stitches. Stuff it and sew it closed. Attach the bead to its crocheted setting by stitching from the back of the crocheted base.

Steps in assembling a crocheted jewelled bead.

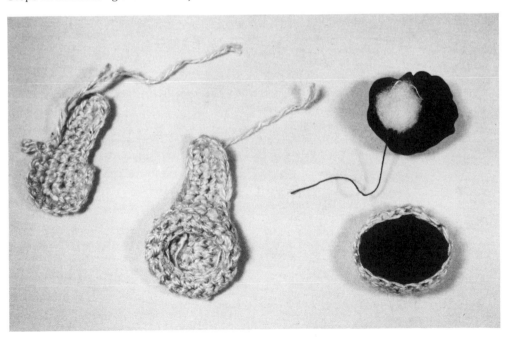

Necklace in bright metallic threads and jewel colors. The chain is a three-cord braid with these components: round commercial cord in variegated green, blue, yellow and red; crocheted cord of green embroidery floss; and crocheted cord of dark-blue silk and metallic threads. The jewel is of red silk, set in a bead crocheted of gold thread.

On this bead, the rectangular tab folds under, providing a loop for the cord to pass through.

SUGGESTED VARIATIONS:
Crocheted and stuffed beads and braids can be combined in an infinite number of ways. The thread used to make the bead should match or harmonize with the threads in the cord. In this necklace, for example, the setting for the bead is crocheted in gold lamé.

Rolled Ribbon Beads

MATERIALS (for each bead):
  7 to 12 inches of fancy ribbon
  White glue, such as Elmer's
  Silk buttonhole twist or sewing thread

TOOLS:
  Pencil
  Clamp clothespin
  Crewel needle (size 7, 8 or 9)

These are the easiest soft beads to make. All that is required is ribbon that is woven tightly enough not to ravel too much. Simply wind the ribbon around a pencil, gluing as you go. Use tiny dabs of Elmer's or a similar white glue for this purpose. Use a clamp clothespin to hold the bead in place until the glue dries. Finish the bead by turning the end under and stitching it carefully to the previous coil of the bead. These beads can then be slipped onto a decorative cord in a contrasting color to make a lovely easy necklace.

SUGGESTED VARIATIONS:
Ribbons rolled in scrolls rather than plain cylinders can be used for connecting two braids, cords or stuffed bias-tape cords. Ribbon scrolls can also be used as the backing for larger, loose beads. For example, you might make a floppy, crocheted leaf form and sew it to the ribbon scroll. This would be a good way to make a dramatic collar in fall colors.

  To make a ring, simply roll the ribbon around a cylinder the same thickness as your finger. Why not make a whole collection of thin rings from ribbon, to be worn all at once?

Steps in assembling rolled ribbon beads.

Stuffed Barrel Beads

MATERIALS:
   Scraps of silk at least 2 × 4 inches for each bead. You might
      want to cut many beads from one larger square of tie-dyed
      silk, cutting the beads around the patterns formed by the
      dye.
   Scrap of linen backing for each bead shape
   Sewing thread
   Polyester fiber stuffing

TOOLS:
   Sewing needle (size 10 or 11)
   Sewing machine

Sew long rectangular pockets from silk backed with handkerchief
linen. If you are making a great many beads, you can sew several
of these rectangles at once and then cut them apart. Use your
machine for this sewing.

   Cut out the rectangles, trim the corners and turn the pockets
inside out. The blunt end of a crochet hook is very useful for this
purpose. Stuff each pocket lightly and slip stitch the end shut.

   Now roll the stuffed rectangle's ends together and stitch the
bead into a barrel shape. You might want to add decorative embroidery to hide this seam and further enhance the bead. The blue
silk beads on page 57 are made in this way, as are the beads in the
stuffed silk necklace.

Steps in making a stuffed barrel bead.

Necklace in gold, turquoise and tangerine silk. The cord is handmade bias tape. A variegated fine cord was used for wrapping.

SUGGESTED VARIATIONS:
To make a ring or bracelet, just make a stuffed barrel bead with a very large central hole. For a bracelet, you will need a piece of cloth about 3 inches longer than the diameter of a comfortable bangle. You can vary the width, or even make your bracelet in a graceful shape.

Knot and loop closures.

CLOSURES

The main requirement for closures is that they actually close, and close securely. Small metal closures such as snaps and hooks and eyes are sold in dime stores. These will work well for many of the pieces in this book. The bracelets on page 81, for instance, all close with tiny snaps.

But on a piece where the closure will have to show, greater attention must be paid to the fine details of the closure. It will then be an integral part of the piece's overall design.

Button and Loop Closure

In this closure, both ends are wrapped in a loop. But on one end, a soft button is sewed, or a bead is strung into the loop. To close, you stuff the bead or button through the other loop. Make sure that the loop is large enough to stuff the bead through but small enough to keep it from sliding out again.

Knot and Loop Closure

This closure is very similar to the button and loop version. But in this case a decorative knot is used as a button. A very fancy knot can be executed by threading cord through a large tapestry needle and weaving the needle in and out of a central knot. The end of the cord should be wrapped to keep it from ravelling and then buried in the knot.

PROJECTS USING BRAIDS, CORDS AND TRIMS

Bias Tape Bracelets

Bias tape bound over drapery cording is very flexible. You can use it to make all kinds of coiled shapes. You might tie-dye yellow bias tape in oranges and browns and use it to make a coiled snake bracelet, headband or armband. The coiled snake pendant in Chapter Four can be used with such an armband.

MATERIALS (for each bracelet):
    Single-fold bias tape strip, about 1 inch longer than the
        circumference of a comfortable bangle bracelet
    Small silk scraps, each about 2 inches square (2 for each bead)
    Silk buttonhole twist (for sewing beads)
    Sewing thread (for sewing bias tape)
    Cotton drapery cording (½-inch size) the same length as the
        bias tape strip (for stuffing bracelet)
    Polyester fiber stuffing (for stuffing beads)
    2 tiny snaps (size 00)

Cotton bracelets made from commercial bias tape stitched over cotton drapery cording. This is a quick, attractive idea for an item to sell.

TOOLS:
   Crewel needle (size 7, 8 or 9)

To make a bias tape bracelet, cut a length of bias tape. The strip should be about one inch longer than the width of a comfortable bangle bracelet. Iron the bias tape if necessary to eliminate the center fold. Then place a length of drapery cord inside the bias tape. Use whip stitches to cover the cord with the bias tape. This procedure is shown in a photograph on page 68.

Sew tiny snaps at the end of the bound tape to use for the bracelet fastener. If you like, you can make cloth beads to slide on the bracelet. The bracelets in this picture are decorated with barrel and rolled ribbon beads (see pages 77 and 78).

SUGGESTED VARIATIONS:
You might try making a bias tape necklace from several fabrics. For example, make short strips of bias tape from brown tweed, green velveteen, heavy brown silk and orange cotton. Arrange these strips in a four-tiered choker.

Stuffed bias tape can be treated like a giant thread and be macraméd, braided or knotted. The necklace in the photo, for example, was made from macraméd and knotted bias tape.

Necklace of polyester cord, tie-dyed and then knotted, braided, and macraméd. The ends are rewoven and then stitched to the back of the piece.

Wrapped Feather Necklace

Wrapped feathers are lovely in conjunction with macramé. A necklace macraméd from thin rope could have some feathers wrapped into the piece itself and other feathers dangling from the loose ends.

MATERIALS:
> 2 equal lengths of braid or cord, about twice as long as the
> finished necklace or belt
> Silk buttonhole twist (for wrapping)
> Pheasant feathers (4 for each end)

TOOLS:
> Crewel needle (size 7, 8 or 9)

To make this feather and cord necklace, lay two pieces of cord side by side. Each piece should be about twice as long as you want the finished necklace to be. Knot the two cords together in a pattern of square knots. In this necklace, I made a double square knot every six inches along the cord.

You will now have two loose ends on each end of the necklace, or four ends in all. You will want to wrap a feather or clump of feathers on each loose end. To attach feathers by wrapping, lay the stems of the feathers next to the cord. Then wrap the wrapping thread tightly around both the cord and the stem. If you are wrapping with fine thread, such as the silk buttonhole twist used here, you may want to use a needle to do the wrapping. Directions for wrapping are included on page 58.

SUGGESTED VARIATIONS:
To make feather earrings, wrap the ends of several feathers separately. Do not cut off the wrapping threads. For each earring, braid together the wrapping threads of three or four feathers. Then loop that braid over the earring finding.

Stuffed Eye Necklace

Scraps of silk left over from other projects can be beautifully recycled into soft jewelry. Tie-dyeing is a simple method to help you recycle. Space does not permit me to give complete instructions for tie-dyeing in this book, but doing this project will give you some experience in tie-dyeing. You will want to do a lot more experimenting on your own.

MATERIALS (for three beads):
    Bias-woven polyester edging (1 fold), twice as long as you
        want your finished necklace to be
    Cotton drapery cording (same length)
    Silk square (about 9 inches square)
    Scrap of linen, the same size as the silk
    Liquid dye
    String for tie-dyeing
    Silk buttonhole twist
    Tissue paper
    Sewing-machine thread
    Snaps or hooks and eyes for fastener

TOOLS:
    Coffee can for dyeing
    Sewing needles
    Sewing machine

Wash the scrap of silk in lukewarm water. Squeeze it out gently until it is damp. Then pinch three bits of cloth at three spots on the cloth. Wrap string tightly around each pinched section. The cloth is now ready to tie-dye.

Pour about a half a capful of liquid dye, such as Rit, into the bottom of a coffee can. Add boiling hot water until the can is about two-thirds full. Then add the tied cloth. How long you leave the cloth in the dye depends on how dark you want your final color to be. The dyed color should look several shades darker than the color you want, as the color will fade as it dries.

For this necklace, I tie-dyed in two layers. I began with cream colored silk. I wrapped three pinched areas and dyed the fabric aqua. Then I added another inch or two of wrapping and dyed the cloth brown. No matter what color combination you use, always dye the lighter color of the fabric under the wrapped area. When

Necklace of synthetic cord, tie-dyed and stitched over cotton drapery cording. Ornamental butterfly knots and tie-dyed tab beads complete the design.

you finish dyeing all the colors, unwrap the strings. Wash the tie-dyed cloth several times in lukewarm water, until the dye stops "bleeding."

Make three tab beads from the silk, placing the pattern so that the eye is in the center of each bead. Use linen for the backs of the beads. Instructions for making tab beads are on page 70.

To make the cord, cut a length of polyester edging, about twice as long as you want your finished necklace to be. Make several overhand knots in the edging. Pull these knots as tight as you can. Then dunk them in the dye with the silk scraps. The areas under each knot will remain the color of the original edging, creating a reptilian effect. Untie the knots under running water, using a spoon handle or crochet hook to work them loose. Bind the edging over cotton drapery cording (instructions are on p. 67). Then re-tie the cord in decorative knots.

SUGGESTED VARIATIONS:
Try tie-dyeing a large silk square in shades of purple, pink and yellow. Tie pebbles into the cloth to achieve dramatic round shapes. When the cloth dries, cut out round beads and make a necklace in flower colors.

Jewelled Choker Necklace

MATERIALS:
  4 equal lengths of braid, cord and thread in various textures
    and colors. Each length should be 4 times the length of the
    finished necklace. One thread should be gold lamé.
  Scrap of silk, about 2 inches square, for each bead
  Silk buttonhole twist (for sewing bead)
  Polyester fiber stuffing (for bead)

TOOLS:
  Tailor's ham or soft workboard
  T-pins
  Crochet hook
  Crewel needle (size 7, 8 or 9)

To make this choker necklace, cut four lengths of braid or cord in various colors and textures. Each length should be about four times as long as you want your finished choker to be.

Braid the four lengths together in a four-cord braid. Instructions for making the braid are on page 58. You will then have one long braid, which should be twice as long as your choker will be.

Fold this braid in half. Thread a crocheted jewel bead (see page

75) on the double braid. Use the looped end of the braid as the loop for your closure. Tie the two loose ends to each other in an elaborate knot. The knot for this necklace is a quadruple square knot. I then use a needle to pass the ends of the various cords into the center of the knot.

If any of the threads or cords you are using is the kind that unravels easily, wrap the ends firmly to keep them in place.

SUGGESTED VARIATIONS:
You can make much more complex versions of this necklace by varying the textures and sizes of the threads, the number of beads and the type of braid. You will find many suggestions in this chapter to help you experiment. For a lovely belt in shell colors, for example, braid coral mohair, crewel wools in shades of pink and orange, and white linen together in a long rope. Make wrapped ridges of nubby white linen. Between the ridges, add other wrapped colors in a pattern. A dark purplish-brown would be good.

4 · Pendants

A PENDANT IS any piece of jewelry that is suspended. Usually a pendant hangs from a cord or chain. Pendants can be suspended from necklaces, bracelets, hair ornaments, earrings or belts. Although the pendant is the focus of such jewelry, the cord, belt or whatever supports the pendant must also be considered in the design.

Pendants offer a number of advantages for needle-made jewelry. Flat pendants are perfect display surfaces for fine embroidery, couching or other needlework. A pendant is a great solution to the problem of what to do with an old embroidered patch, a bit of petit point, or even a small crocheted doily.

An important part of each pendant in this chapter is the system of loops on the back. You can sew the loops in such a way that you can wear the same pendant on a necklace, a bracelet or a belt.

The back of the pendant should lie flat against the body. If you like, you can add a small pocket on the back. Your pendant can then become a small neck bag.

The front of the pendant can be any fantastic shape you like. Stuffing, quilting, coiling and appliqué are just a few of the techniques you can use to give pendants dimension.

Antique embroidered silk pendant from China. The anonymous artisan worked the grape design in tiny silk knots. The base fabric is wine red; the grapes are green and purple; and the cords and tassels are orange. (From Port of Entry, Chicago.)

Butterfly pendant worked in satin stitch on gold handkerchief linen. The butterfly is shaded in blues, greens, yellows and browns. Notice how I used a decorated running-stitch trim both to attach the bias tape and to make it harmonize more closely with the embroidery.

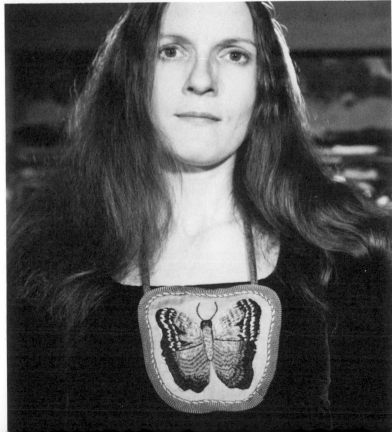

Stuffed Grape Pendant

MATERIALS:
Untreated cotton, about ¼ yard
Wax crayons in blues, purples and greens
Liquid dye (Rit)
Stacks of newspapers
Polyester fiber stuffing
Sewing thread (purple and green)
Small scrap of felt (purple)
Waxed linen thread (for necklace cord)

TOOLS:
Coffee cans for dyeing
Iron
Candle
Sewing machine
Embroidery scissors
Sewing needles (sizes 9, 10 or 11)

This project uses a simple version of batik, a very old textile technique. Batik is a method of resist-dyeing. Wax is melted onto the fabric in a pattern. The cloth is then dyed. The waxed areas resist the dye; therefore, when the wax is removed, those sections retain the fabric's original color.

In crayon batik, melted wax crayons are used to draw the design. Since the colors in the crayons themselves are not removed with the wax, the crayons act both as the resist and as coloring agents. Only one dye bath is necessary.

Crayon batik is not really suitable for large pieces of clothing, but for small items that do not need to be cleaned often, it is an exciting medium.

Trace the leaf shape and cut it out of a piece of light cardboard. Trace four leaves on your fabric. On another piece of fabric, with a dark crayon, trace eight circles about four inches in diameter, using a mug or small plate for a pattern.

Spread a thick pad of newspaper over your work surface. Melted wax is very messy, so dress accordingly. To color on the cloth, soften a wax crayon in a candle flame. When the wax begins to run, stroke the crayon designs onto the cloth. Work as quickly as possible.

Be sure to hold the candle over an area outside the traced

shapes. Otherwise, the places where the candle drips will make spots that will remain the color of the original fabric.

Drip the candle deliberately in spots where you want the ground fabric to show through. The sun spots on these grapes were made with dripped candle wax.

When the crayon dries, soak the pieces of cloth in cool water.

Pattern for the leaf shape.

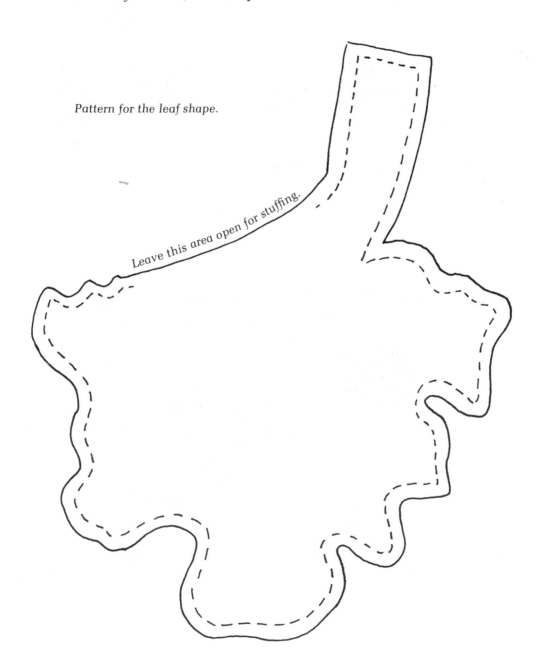

Leave this area open for stuffing.

The grape leaves traced on the fabric and decorated with softened crayons.

Dyeing the grapes in a coffee can.

The water hardens the wax and makes the fabric more receptive to the dye.

While the fabric is soaking, pour green and purple liquid dye into coffee cans. Use a capful or two of dye and fill the coffee can about two-thirds full. Use *cool* water, to avoid melting or softening the wax.

Squeeze out the fabric gently. Some of your wax will crackle, so be as gentle as you can.

Dump the damp fabric in the dye. Let it sit for at least ten minutes—longer if you want a deeper color. The color of the wet dyed fabric should be much darker than the color you want for the final piece, as some color will fade during rinsing and drying.

Remove the pieces of cloth from the cans and rinse them out in cool water until the water runs clear. Hang the pieces up to dry. (A caution from sad experience: Do not lay the cloth on a radiator or near a stove so that it will dry faster; the wax will run and ruin the design. This is the sort of mistake everyone makes at least once.)

When the cloth is dry, place it between several sheets of newspaper. Iron out the wax with a very hot iron. You will have to iron

Ironing out the wax.

The evolution of the grape cluster.

many times to get all the wax out. Keep changing the newspaper so that the colors won't blot into each other.

Even after all the wax is out, the fabric will be rather stiff. This stiffness is desirable in most jewelry. It can be removed completely with repeated washing, although some of your color will fade as well.

Cut the circles and leaf shapes out of the batiked fabric. To make a grape, make a row of running stitches around the outer edge of the circle. Pull the thread to gather the circle into a ball. Fill the ball with stuffing. Then pull the thread tight and knot it firmly. Cut a small oval patch from felt. With overhand (hem) stitches, sew the felt patch over the gathered hole. Make eight grapes in this manner.

Arrange seven of the grapes in a cluster. Save the remaining grape for the necklace closure. Sew the grapes together on the back side, using overhand stitches.

Pin the leaves together in pairs, right sides facing in. Sew each pair together about ⅓ inch from the edge. Sewing curved edges by machine is easy if you go very slowly and make frequent stops, lifting the presser foot on each turn. Be sure to leave the flat edge of the leaf open for stuffing.

Make small clips along every curved edge of the leaves. Clip in only as far as the seam—don't cut through the thread. Extra-sharp embroidery scissors are necessary for this operation. Clipping helps the fabric give on the curves; thus the leaves will retain

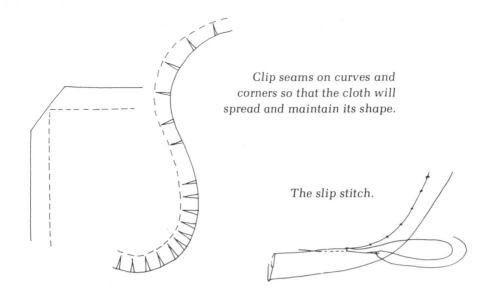

Clip seams on curves and corners so that the cloth will spread and maintain its shape.

The slip stitch.

their rounded edges when they are turned inside out. The small V shapes on this pattern show where to snip.

Turn the leaf right side out and stuff it. Sew the opening closed with slip stitches. A slip stitch in sewing is a stitch that slips through the seam so that no thread shows on the outside of the cloth.

Quilt a design on the leaves with small running stitches. Stitch

Stuffing the grape leaves.

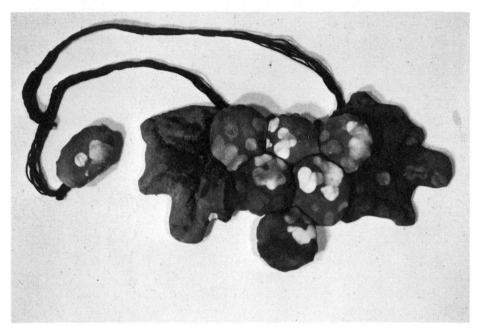

The finished grape pendant. I made the vine by twisting and then wrapping waxed linen thread. An extra grape was used for the button-and-loop closure.

through the stuffing and through both layers of fabric. Your quilting stitches should follow the crayoned design.

Attach the leaves to the grape cluster with overhand stitches. Use double thread and backtrack along the seam for extra strength. Fold the tabs of the grape leaves over, forming loops. You will thread the "vine" through these two loops to hang the necklace.

SUGGESTED VARIATIONS:
Make extra grape beads to use in earrings. Attach the stuffed beads to the earring finding with overcast stitches like those you used for the bead closing.

You can use this same leaf pattern to make large tab beads. String several of these beads on a cord made from brown stuffed bias tape. You can make a leafy necklace or a wreath of leaves for your forehead.

Feathered Nest Pendant

You can change the shape of this pendant to flatter your particular figure (see section on shapes in Chapter One).

MATERIALS:
    15 to 20 pheasant feathers
    Piece of medium-weight garment leather, about 12 inches
        square
    2 tiny scraps of very thin lambskin suede
    Glue
    Silk embroidery twist

TOOLS:
    Awl (for punching sewing holes)
    Large crewel needle (size 5 or 6)
    Heavy shears (do not use good dressmaking shears)

Gluing feathers onto the leather backing.

Any piece of jewelry made with feathers should feature the feathers. They are usually so attractive they will dominate the design anyway. The patterns and colors of a feather are too beautiful to compete with. Work with one feather at a time so that you display each feather to its greatest advantage.

I planned this pendant as the buckle for the thin leather belt shown with it on page 23. You might prefer it on a necklace. The knotted cord on page 62, with feathers wrapped on the ends, would be a nice complement.

To make the pendant, cut two small ovals of equal size from medium-weight leather. Put a large dab of Elmer's or other white glue in the center of the smooth side of one oval.

Glue on the feathers in a half circle. Glue one feather at a time. Glue a small leather patch across this first row of feather stems for reinforcement. Then glue on another row of feathers so that they overlap the leather patch. Glue down a final leather patch so that none of the stems show.

Cover the pendant with newspapers and weight it with a book for at least twenty minutes, or until the glue is completely dry.

The front and back of the pendant, showing the holes punched for sewing.

The double running stitch.

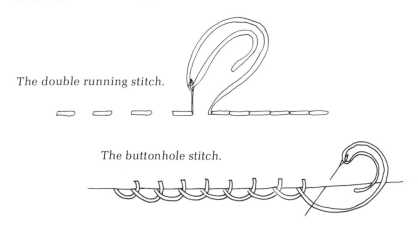

The buttonhole stitch.

Buttonhole stitches worked in double running stitches form the base loops for needle lace.

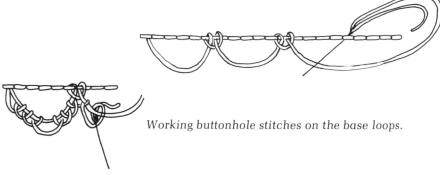

Working buttonhole stitches on the base loops.

When the glue is dry, place the two ovals back to back, smooth, or finished, side out. Punch the sewing holes through both ovals with a small awl or a sailmaker's needle. Clamp clothespins are handy for holding the ovals in place as you punch. Punch a row of holes around the edge of the top oval on the front, as well as on the loop on the back. The holes should be about one-quarter inch apart.

Sew the leather ovals together back to back. For this pendant, I used dark-green silk buttonhole twist and a size 4 crewel needle. I sewed the pieces with a double running stitch. For this stitch, you sew each row twice. On the second sewing, you fill in the spaces in the previous row.

To focus the viewer's eye on the pendant, I made two small egg shapes in a light color of fine leather. They are stuffed with poly-

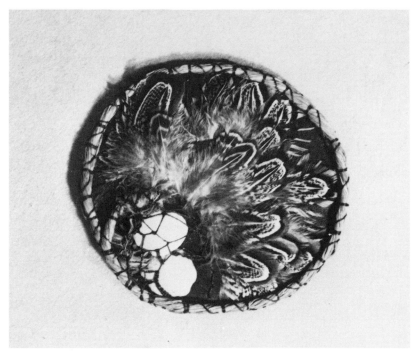

The finished pendant, showing the fiber frame, the stuffed bead shapes and the needle lace.

ester fiber and lightly glued to the dark backing. With the dark-green silk, I then worked a web of needle-lace stitches over the shapes. The basic stitch of needle lace is the buttonhole stitch. Another needle-lace project in this book is the coral reef collar on page 123.

The frame of this pendant was made from natural grasses twisted into a coil. Each of the three layers of the coil was wrapped to the one below it, thus building up a shallow, basket-shaped edge. I used a threaded needle to do the wrapping. If you don't have natural grasses to twist, try using thin rope or rough cord such as baling twine.

SUGGESTED VARIATIONS:
Small, flat, circular pendants like this one can be used like large tab beads. You might want to make several feathered nests, each about two inches across, and string them on a macraméd rope

belt. Small ovals can also be attached to large bobby pins and worn in the hair. Just slide the bobby pin through a leather loop on the back of the pendant.

To make a locket, cut four leather ovals. Use two ovals for the front and two for the back. The loop for hanging the pendant should be on the back of the locket; the feathered design should be glued on the front. Attach the front and back only at the top. You can embroider a small picture inside, or sew in an old watch.

This modern leather necklace from Africa illustrates two basic stitches for working with leather—the double running stitch and the whip stitch, which is the same as an overcast stitch. (From Scarab, Chicago.)

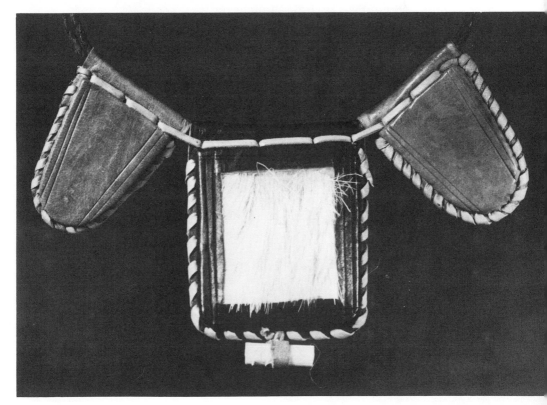

Embroidered Butterfly Sachet Pendant

If you are an experienced embroiderer, you might want to work the butterfly in satin stitch, as I did in the necklace pictured on page 106.

MATERIALS:
   Handkerchief linen (9-inch square)
   2 squares of tangerine-colored silk, each about 6 inches square
   2 squares of nonwoven interfacing, each about 6 inches square
   Tissue paper
   Dressmaker's carbon
   Silk buttonhole twist in shades of gray
   Narrow (¼-inch) polyester ribbon, about 24 inches
   Medium (½-inch) polyester ribbon, about 12 inches
   Decorative metallic ribbon (24 inches)
   Round silver cord (24 inches)

TOOLS:
   Embroidery hoop (6-inch size)
   Crewel needle (size 7, 8 or 9)
   Sewing machine
   Pencil

A sachet is a small pocket or pouch in which fragrant herbs or spices are kept. Victorian young ladies wore embroidered sachets on neck ribbons. The sachets were filled with potpourri, dried rose leaves or other natural perfumes.

This sachet is a pendant. Its back has a vertical slit, into which you insert a small muslin drawstring bag stuffed with herbs. The inside of the pendant has several layers to stiffen the piece and provide a pocket.

Begin by picking a small motif to embroider. The butterflies on pages 104–05 were designed to be worked in satin stitch. Satin stitches are medium-length running stitches worked right next to each other. The stitches lie flat and create a velvety effect.

I did this embroidery with silk buttonhole twist in shades of gray on white handkerchief linen. For a touch of color, I backed the linen with tangerine-colored silk.

Trace your design and use dressmaker's carbon to transfer it to

The satin stitch.

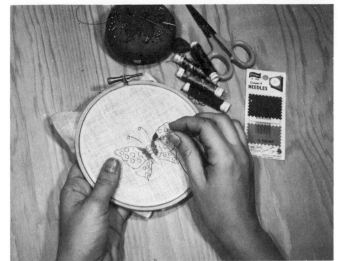

Embroidering the butterfly.

Framing the embroidery
with ribbon.

Sewing the backing and
interfacing.

Patterns for embroidered butterflies.

your ground fabric. Embroider the design through both the ground fabric and the backing fabric. If you are using heavier linen, no backing fabric is necessary.

When you finish the embroidery, wash, dry and press the square. The washing removes the traces of the carbon.

Put the embroidery in a hoop and baste in thin ribbons to make a frame around the design. I used a decorated running stitch to tack the ribbons down.

From a piece of tissue paper, cut the final shape you want your pendant to be. It can be a square or rectangle but should be large enough to include the framed design. Place this pattern on top of the framed embroidery. Cut out the shape.

Cut the same shape from interfacing, from another piece of colored silk, and from a heavy fabric such as linen. You should now have three cut pieces of material and the embroidered design, all in the same shape.

The linen forms the back of the pendant. Sew ribbons on in vertical strips, leaving loops in the same place on each strip for cords to pass through. If you make two or more loops on each

The finished pendant. Note the finishing details: the rolled ribbon beads and decorative knots on the cord, and the decorated running stitches used to attach the ribbon trim.

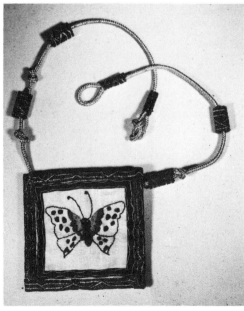

More Chinese embroidered sachets. (From the Field Museum, Chicago.)

vertical strip, you can vary the ways the sachet can be worn. Again, I used decorated running stitches to attach the ribbon.

Now cut the linen piece down the middle and bind the edges with more ribbon. This slit will form the opening for the sachet bag.

To finish the pendant, make a sandwich of the embroidery, interfacing, lining (the colored silk) and the linen back. Baste the layers together, first by hand and then by machine. Bind the outer edges with fancy ribbon, and use the same ribbon to make rolled ribbon beads for the cord.

SUGGESTED VARIATIONS:
Embroidered pendants are perfect for petit point, needlepoint and crewel work. You can embroider small patches with your favorite birds, flowers or other designs. Vary the shape of the pendant to flatter your face. A pendant is a good place to use small embroidered patches you pick up in import stores or on your travels.

Coiled Snake Pendant

Couching is a favorite embroidery technique of mine, providing a wonderful way to add texture to a piece. It allows one to use threads or cords that are too thick or nubby to pass through cloth. Instead, one tacks the cords to the cloth with decorative stitches. A beautiful example of couching is the Afghanistani bag on page 149.

MATERIALS:
    Silk square, at least 12 inches square
    Liquid dye
    String
    Tissue paper
    Smooth ¼-inch shiny cord (for snake)
    Silk buttonhole twist (for couching)
    Heavy interfacing
    Bias tape or ribbon, about 16 inches
    Tiny snaps (size 00)

TOOLS:
    Embroidery hoop (6-inch size)
    Sewing machine
    Crewel needle (size 8 or 9)

I made this pendant from the same piece of tie-dyed silk that I used to make the bias tape in Chapter Three. That tape is used to bind the pendant's edges. The cord used on this pendant is a thin, smooth polyester braid, tie-dyed in copper and brown to give it a more reptilian appearance.

To make the snake, cut a piece of cord about 15 inches long. Fold over the end of the cord and wrap it to keep it from ravelling. This wrapped end will form the center of your first coil.

Coil the cord around itself, fastening each coil to the adjacent one with small overhand stitches. A tailor's ham makes a useful base for this work. Use pins to hold the cord in place as you coil. When you finish coiling, wrap the other end and bury it under a coil.

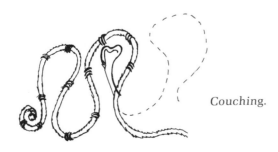

Couching.

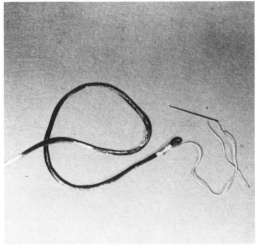 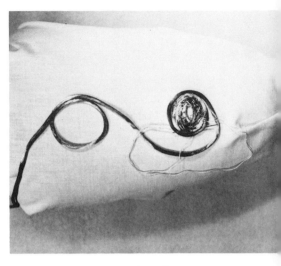

Beginning the coil by wrapping the end.   Sewing the coil on a tailor's ham.

The finished coil couched onto tie-dyed gold silk, which is backed by
medium-weight linen.

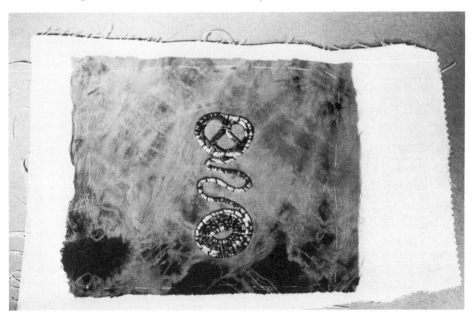

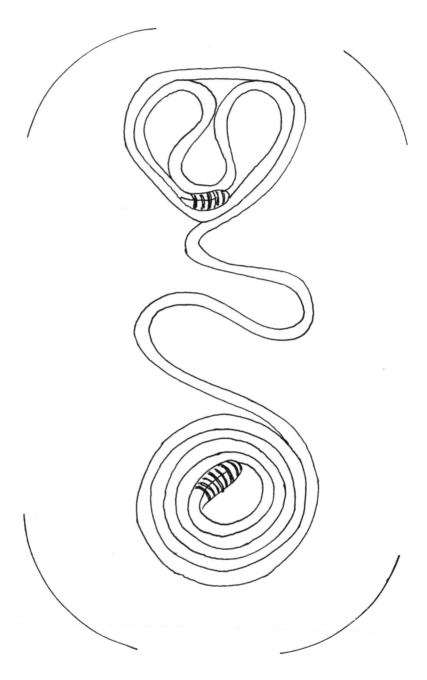

Pattern for the coiling on the snake pendant.

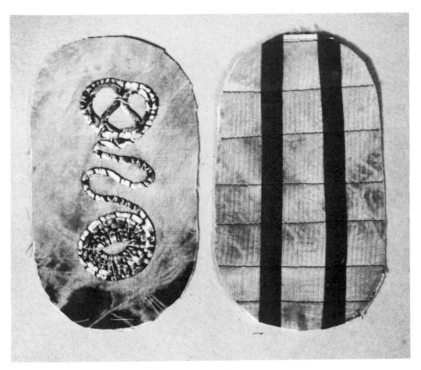

The front and back of the pendant, ready to sew together.

Baste the silk fabric to medium-weight linen. Stretch both layers in an embroidery hoop. Attach the coiled shape to the base with couching stitches. A couching stitch is simply a running stitch worked over the threads to be couched. Work two or three stitches at each spot for strength. The couching stitches should form part of the design. In this example, I have spaced the stitches to create a pattern on the snake's back. I used red, royal blue and gold silk buttonhole twist to do the couching.

Cut out the final shape of the pendant from the linen-backed silk. Cut the same shape from heavy interfacing, another piece from linen, and another from gold silk.

Baste the silk, linen and interfacing together to make the back piece. Baste and then sew strips of ribbon to make loops that will serve as a threading mechanism for a cord or braid.

This pendant can be worn as a belt, an armband, a bracelet or a necklace, depending on how the cord is coiled through the back loops.

SUGGESTED VARIATIONS:

You can couch thick, fuzzy yarns, metallic threads and braids onto fabrics that are relatively delicate, for stunning effects. For example, you might make another version of the feathered nest pendant on page 97 by couching thin rope onto green velveteen. For a medieval collar, try couching gold and silver metallic cord onto red or blue velvet.

The finished pendant worn as an armband. The bracelet is made like a small, stiff belt (see Chapter Six). The pendant is bound with silk bias tape.

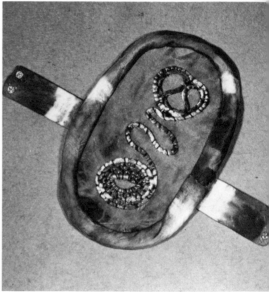

Mountain Landscape Pendant

A pendant is the perfect place to embroider an unforgettable scene from a vacation or a motif to celebrate a birthday, anniversary or other special event. The appliquéd scene on this pendant should suggest many ideas.

MATERIALS:
    Small scraps of silk, velveteen and lace
    Machine embroidery thread
    Single-fold bias tape (about 24 inches)
    Round silky cord (about 12 inches)
    2 squares of cotton velveteen (about 9 inches square)
    Nonwoven heavy interfacing (9-inch square)

TOOLS:
    Sewing machine with zigzag stitch
    Crewel needle (size 7, 8 or 9)

Your first step will be to choose and arrange your fabrics to reflect the image you have in mind. I made this pendant from scraps of turquoise, brown and gray tie-dyed silk left over from a previous project.

If you are inexperienced at tie-dyeing, by the way, it is less expensive than you might think. Practice on small squares of silk, since the silk takes dye so beautifully, and almost every scrap of material dyed at one session can be used in this piece of jewelry.

To make this pendant, you might also want to use sewing scraps. Small cotton prints such as those used for quilting are especially suitable. Scraps of lace and old trims can add finishing touches.

Rearrange and cut your scraps until your scene begins to take shape. The peaks of the mountains in this picture were suggested to me by the waves of the tie-dyeing. Then I found a scrap of velveteen to use for the lake—I liked the contrast of textures between the velveteen and the silk.

For trims I used ordinary "silk" bias binding—actually polyester—which can be found in any dime store. To make the snowflakes, I used scraps of lace that had a six-point design.

Incidentally, I sewed every tiny scrap of silk to handkerchief linen before working with it, and I kept rebasting as I snipped.

Assembling tie-dyed scraps, bits of lace, and trim.

Basting the pieces to the base cloth.

The scene, embroidered by machine and trimmed with bias tape.

There really isn't a shorter, easier way to keep small pieces of silk steady as you work.

When you have arranged your scene, baste the cut shapes to a ground fabric. I used another piece of tie-dyed silk for the background. This, too, I tacked onto handkerchief linen. Baste a little way in from the edge so that your machine stitching will not cover the basting stitches.

When your shapes are tightly anchored, appliqué them to the ground fabric. You can use zigzag machine stitches, as I did, or work satin stitches by hand. Other possibilities include appliquéing with slip stitches, using decorated running stitches, or covering up the stitching with couched threads. You will see examples of these other techniques for appliqué in other parts of this book.

Trim your scene into the final shape. Cut a layer of interfacing the same size as the scene. Bind the scene and the interfacing together with bias tape.

Place this framed scene in the center of a larger oval of fabric. Frame the scene with couched cord. The couching also attaches the small oval to the larger one.

Now cut large ovals of interfacing and heavy linen for backing.

Sew threading loops and, if you like, a large pocket on the linen back.

This pendant has a loop that allows it to be worn as a necklace. It also has two hooks and eyes, which can be used to attach it to the lace on the Victorian collar described on page 119.

SUGGESTED VARIATIONS:
Do a bit of needlework to commemorate a birth, anniversary or special event. Then mount the needlework on heavy interfacing. Arrange the loops on the back of the pendant so that the piece can be used as a belt, necklace, armband or bracelet.

Why not do a needlepoint charm necklace for your favorite grandmother? Add a new small pendant for each grandchild.

The finished pendant, trimmed with couched cord and bias tape.

5 · Collars

A COLLAR IS a piece of clothing as well as a piece of jewelry. A collar should be made in a shape flattering to the face, since it serves as a kind of frame for the face. In fact, a collar is often the ideal solution to the problem of a dress with an unflattering neckline.

The mountain landscape pendant worn on a basic round collar creates a Victorian look.

Removable collars were very popular in previous eras, but today this elegant tradition has been somewhat lost. One reason might be that women in past eras owned much less clothing than we do today. Thus a woman might have had one basic "best" dress, which she could vary with her collars. With the prices of clothes going up as they are, this remains a very sensible system.

When we think of collars we frequently think of lace. The lace collars extant in museums are amazingly intricate and luxurious. It isn't likely that you will have the patience to work lace stitches in fine thread. But you can experiment with lacemaking techniques in heavier fibers.

In this book you have already learned a variety of other techniques that could be used to make collars. For example, you might make a collar of coiled shapes on a silk background, or of small feather and leather shapes connected by coiled and wrapped cords.

Victorian Collar

A soft, dark collar is a wonderful place to display antique jewelry, bits of old lace and other treasures. Collars can be made in many shapes. But the center of any collar is a circle—the hole provided for the wearer's neck. Thus the easiest collar is simply a large, flat circle of cloth. This shape can be lengthened into an oval or sharpened into a V. But whatever the shape, the design should point to the neck and face.

MATERIALS:
   Printed cotton velveteen (½ yard)
   Nonwoven interfacing, medium weight (½ yard)
   2-inch lace (½ yard)
   Sewing thread
   Single-fold bias tape (about 1 yard)

TOOLS:
   Sewing machine
   Sewing needle (size 10 or 11)

To make this Victorian collar, draw two concentric circles on a large piece of lightweight polyester interfacing, using a compass. The radius of the smaller circle should be the same as the distance between your Adam's apple and the point on your shoulder where you want your collar to begin. The outer circle can be as large as you want it. You can make your shoulders appear wider or narrower by varying the width of the collar.

   Cut around the circumference of the larger circle. Pin and baste this interfacing to the wrong side of your ground fabric. The ground fabric that I used for this project was a lightweight Italian velveteen in subtle gray, green, blue and cream patterned stripes. Any fairly strong fabric will do. If you work with a lighter fabric, such as silk, be sure to back the entire ground fabric with tissue paper before basting and then cutting out the circle.

   Make sure that the center front and center back of your collar are aligned on the grain of the fabric—that is, in the direction of the lengthwise threads of the weave. Otherwise your collar will stretch out of shape.

   Cut the collar shape out of the ground fabric. You will need to cut another collar shape for the backing. This can be cut from the

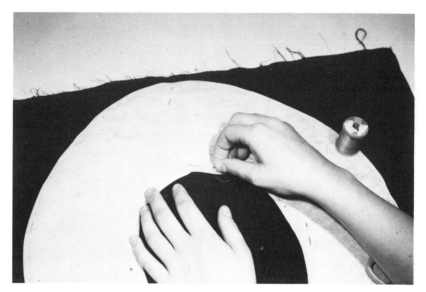

Basting the interfacing onto the back side of the fabric.

Trimming the front of the collar with lace.

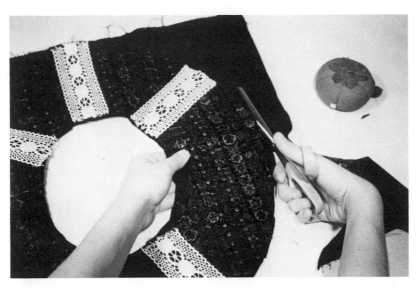

Using the front of the collar as the pattern for the back.

same fabric as the front or from fabric in a contrasting color. You can make a reversible collar by binding the edges with bias trim.

Heavy linen is a good fabric to use for the backing of a collar. In fact, if you use linen you might want to dispense with the interfacing. How many layers you use depends on how stiff you want your collar to be.

Trim the front of the collar with lace or other trim. Baste the trim on before you tack it down by machine.

Incidentally, the oval hole from this collar forms the base for the pendant on page 116. The pendant can be suspended from the collar with a hook and eye or a button and loop, or worn by itself.

Use single-fold bias tape to finish the collar. Sew one side of the tape all around the edges of the collar, using your sewing machine. Then fold the tape to the back side and hemstitch it in place.

SUGGESTED VARIATIONS:
To add a ruffle to the edge of the collar, cut your fabric in diagonal strips, as you do for making bias tape (see Index of Techniques). Connect the diagonal strips to make a long, unfolded bias tape. Make a small hem on one side of the bias tape. Gather the other

This child's collar (from the Field Museum in Chicago) is very cleverly designed. Its base is essentially a basic round collar. But the patchwork is designed in such a way that the tiger appears to be draped over the child's shoulder when the collar is worn. Perhaps this collar will give you ideas for other imaginative animal designs.

side with running stitches and sew it around the bottom of the collar.

You might also want to make a fairly small collar and add a long ruffle of 6-inch lace.

Collars can be made in any shape. See Chapter One for suggestions on how to shape the collar to flatter your face.

Coral Reef Collar

The gorgeous needle laces of Europe, such as Chantilly, were made with the same stitch I used in this collar.

MATERIALS:
 Nubby linen yarn in 2 shades of gray (1 skein each)
 Silk scraps in 2 shades of tangerine (each about 9 inches square)
 Tissue paper
 Polyester fiber stuffing
 Silk buttonhole twist

TOOLS:
 Soft workboard
 Crochet hook (size G or H)
 Blunt tapestry needle
 T-pins

A collar may be nothing more than a group of pendants and beads connected together. This collar uses crocheted and stuffed bead shapes similar to the ones described in Chapter Three. But instead of being strung on a cord, the shapes here are connected into a continuous fabric by needle lace.

Needle lace is an openwork version of the buttonhole stitch in embroidery. You can see drawings of the basic needle-lace stitch on page 99.

For the crocheted shapes in this collar, I used slubbed linen yarn in a soft, silvery gray. The stuffed sections are made of dark and light coral silk. The lace is worked in white linen thread.

Begin by working several free-form shapes in crochet.

Work a base of single crochets and then stitch up walls of crochet to make cups for beads as described in Chapter Three. To

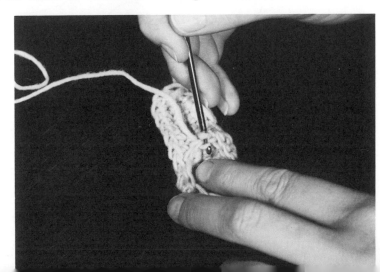

Making free-form crocheted shapes.

Patterns for the free-form crocheted shapes of the coral reef collar.

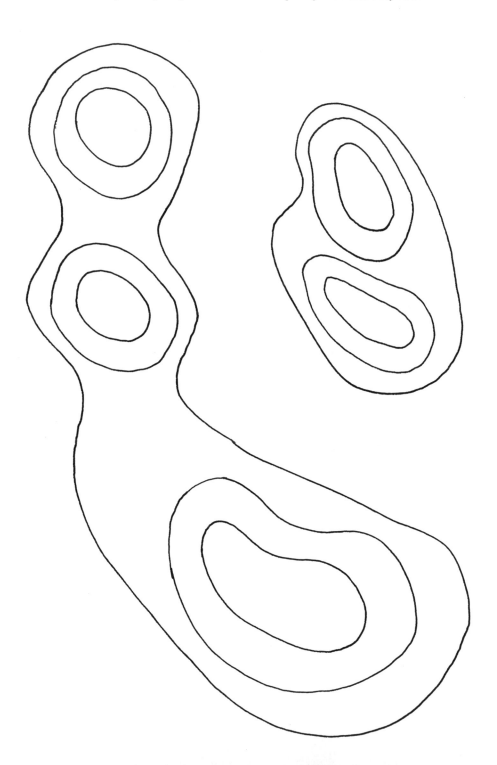

turn corners and keep a piece flat, work extra single crochets in the corner holes. To make a shape curve up, decrease the stitches around the outer edges.

If you like, you can begin with a general pattern of what your forms will look like. Keep holding the forms up to the pattern as you crochet. The drawing shows the pattern I used in making the coral necklace. Your final shapes may not fit those shapes exactly. You can, and probably will, make variations in your design as you work.

To make these shapes, I crocheted a small, flat oval shape about the size of the base of a cloth bead. I then built up a little wall or cup of stitches to form the central cavity.

I tied off the crocheting at the top edge of the wall and then began crocheting again at the base of the shape. In this way I built up concentric walls.

When you have finished your crocheted shapes, arrange them in a pleasing formation. The inner part of your arrangement should be the ring for your neck.

Use T-pins to attach the crocheted shapes to a soft workboard. Then cut scraps from silk and make stuffed beads to fill in the cavities in the crocheted forms. Sew the beads to the bases of the crocheted pieces.

Thread a tapestry needle with the thread that you have chosen for the lace. Any thread that is tightly spun and therefore strong will do. Lacemaking thread should not be too fuzzy or unevenly textured or you will have problems working with it. But some unevenness is often desirable. Experiment with small pieces of needle lace before deciding on the best thread to use. You will want to use thread that contrasts somewhat in texture with the thread you used for the crochet.

Tie one end of your thread to the underside of a crocheted

Arranging the shapes on the workboard.

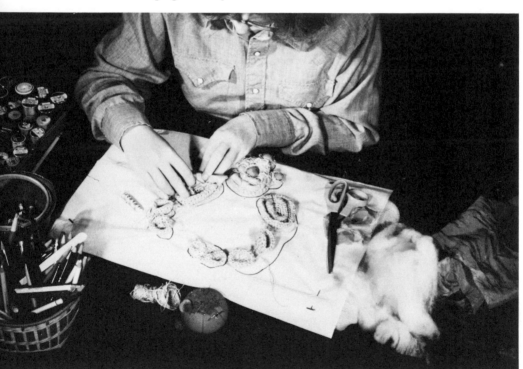

The stuffed shapes connected by needle lace.

Making the basic needle-lace stitch.

The weaver's knot.

shape. Then pass the thread to an edge. Work buttonhole stitches in the loops of the crochet stitches, all around the edges of the forms. Then go back and work more buttonhole stitches in the loops of the first row of buttonhole stitches. You can vary the length of the loops to form a lace design.

When you run out of thread, don't knot it to the base again. Instead, use a weaver's knot to connect it to the next thread. Snip the ends close to the knot. The knot will disappear among the knots of the lace.

To make a scallop or frill in the lace, make long loops with the thread. You might connect two crocheted forms with just such a loop. Then reinforce the loop by working buttonhole stitches on that base thread. On the next row, connect loops along the base thread. Study the photograph of the collar to see the loops that grow naturally from needle lace.

The closure for this collar is a variation of the button-and-loop closure. A long loop of needle lace fastens over one of the stuffed-bead buttons.

SUGGESTED VARIATIONS:
In the elaborate laces of pre-industrial Europe, each stitch was carefully counted to form elegant floral and scroll designs. After

The finished collar.

To make this feather collar, I cut a basic round collar from a piece of leather and a narrower shape from softer leather. The string of feathers was glued in a sandwich between them. I then tacked on the braid with double running stitches. The stitches anchored the feathers even more firmly.

you have experimented with lace in free form, you might want to try doing a counted-stitch pattern.

You might want to make a stiff collar base like that of the Victorian collar and work the needle lace right on that base. On a dark-green velvet base, you could work needle lace in ecru linen thread, working in little bits of cloth, small crocheted beads, small stuffed forms or little metallic threads.

A needle-lace collar, particularly if it is free form, should not be matched to other jewelry. But though a coral headdress would look ridiculous worn with this collar, it might well look spectacular with a long, flowing robe. You could also make coral reef forms that encircle your arms or ankles.

6 · Belts

FOR THOUSANDS OF YEARS, human clothing consisted primarily of the loose tunic covered with a variety of flowing mantles, collars, cloaks and robes. In those times the belt was a wardrobe item that received a great deal of attention. Museums contain lovely examples of belts from Greek, Roman, Byzantine, Celtic and later eras. These belts were often designed to carry money, jewels and other valuables. Belts are important symbols in literature and mythology—they were seen as conferring magic powers or making the wearer immune from harm.

Belts are not as important to our wardrobe today. Even men's

The diamond "eye of God" is only one of the design motifs in this Bolivian belt. (From the collection of the author.)

Cummerbund of stuffed, appliquéd and quilted silk, embroidered in silk buttonhole twist.

Belt of crewel wool embroidered on black wool. Patterns for embroidering both the belt and the grape bag are included in this book.

clothing is less reliant on them than in the past. In modern fashion, belts are used more often to accent costumes than to call attention to themselves. Some belts are thin cords or chains whose light weight holds the fabric in soft, loose folds—the belt rests on the hips instead of cinching the waist. The cords you learned to make in Chapter Three can all be used to make belts such as these.

In this chapter you will learn how to make more substantial belts—belts that have shape and body.

A belt usually has two parts—the belt itself and its buckle. The buckles of needle-made belts are essentially pendants. The pendant can slide on the belt or be permanently attached to one end of it, where it covers a fastener. Of course, you can also buy a metal buckle and sew it to a fabric belt.

Basic Ribbon Belt

MATERIALS:
  2-inch metallic ribbon, 3 inches longer than the wearer's waist
      circumference
  Belt stiffening, the same length as the ribbon
  2-inch grosgrain ribbon, the same length as the front ribbon
  7 pieces of ribbon in various widths, patterns and colors, each
      6 inches long
  Heavy nonwoven interfacing (6 inches square)
  Large hook and eye
  Machine embroidery thread
  Silk buttonhole twist (for sewing on fasteners)

TOOLS:
  Sewing machine (size 16 needle)
  Crewel needle (size 7, 8 or 9)

This is a basic belt of thin ribbon that fits around the waist or rests on the hips. This belt can be soft or stiff, depending on the way you want to use it. In general, the wider the belt, the more layers of stiffening it should have, to keep it from rolling up. Even leather, the most common material for belts, sometimes needs stiffening.

The belt shown is made from pieces of ribbon. But a straight, narrow belt can be made from almost any material. Crewel work makes beautiful belts, as do needlepoint and petit point. For needlepoint, one layer of stiffening is usually sufficient, since the stitching has thickened the fabric so much already. You will probably want to sew a needlepoint belt by hand rather than on the machine. Light quilting is another lovely way to work a design on a belt.

The design for your ribbon belt will begin right at the ribbon counter. Lay the ribbons next to each other and experiment with colors and textures. For stability, it is a good idea to alternate brocaded ribbons (those with loose threads "floating" on the reverse side) with velvet, grosgrain or other more tightly woven ribbons. Ribbons with metallic thread in them are especially nice for jewelry.

To make this belt, you will need seven short pieces of ribbon for the buckle and one long ribbon to go around your waist. You will also need one or more layers of belt backing and a piece of

The parts of a belt sandwich. Add more layers if you want a stiffer belt.

grosgrain ribbon the same size as the ribbon to be used around your waist.

The basic belt is put together like a sandwich. First comes the outer layer, the decorated surface of the belt. In the middle come layers of backing (stiffening or interfacing). Belt backing can be bought at fabric counters in different widths and weights. Canvas webbing is also useful for this purpose. The weight of your backing will depend on the material you have used for the belt. The

The finished backing and fastenings on the ribbon belt and the crewel belt. On the crewel belt, I added two extra layers of interfacing.

The finished ribbon belt.

heavier the ribbon, the heavier the backing should be. The belt must also have an inner layer, so that the interfacing and stiffening will not show.

How you fasten the layers together depends on your materials. I basted the layers of this ribbon belt together by hand and then sewed them on the machine. For the crewelwork belt, I basted the black wool to heavy black interfacing and then bound both those layers over a stiff backing. I attached the grosgrain ribbon lining with decorated running stitches.

To make the ribbon buckle, sew the ribbons side by side on a piece of heavy interfacing, basting them first by hand and then anchoring them on the machine. Then fold the interfacing in half, with the ribbons facing in. Sew a seam across the bottom of the ribbons. Turn the buckle inside out, slide the end of the belt in, and sew the narrow ends of the buckle down over the belt. The buckle hides a large hook-and-eye fastener.

SUGGESTED VARIATIONS:
Sew a ribbon purse (see Chapter Seven) to slide along a ribbon belt. The chapter on pendants explains how to make the sliding mechanism. Ribbon belts can be used to make strong handles for little bags you wear around your neck.

Ribbons can also be interwoven for unusual designs and textures.

Crewel Grape Belt

Crewel works beautifully for accessories meant for wool outfits.

MATERIALS:
    Black wool hopsacking (¼ yard)
    Tissue paper
    Dressmaker's carbon (white)
    Crewel wools in greens, pinks and purples
    Belt stiffener, about 3 inches longer than the circumference of
        your waist
    Grosgrain ribbon, 2 inches wide and the same length as the
        stiffening
    Sewing thread
    Hook and eye

TOOLS:
    Pencil
    Embroidery hoop
    Crewel needles (size depends on number of strands used)

To make the crewel belt, cut a long piece of wool or linen, at least six inches longer than and twice as wide as you want your fin-

Pattern for the embroidery on the crewel belt.

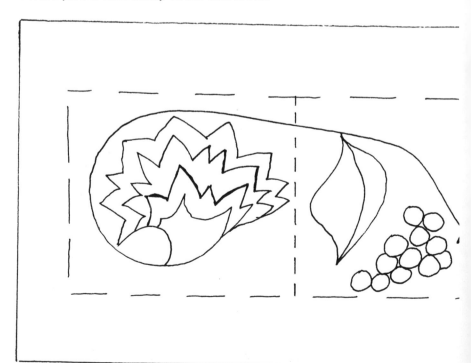

The crewel grape belt.

ished belt to be. The more excess fabric you have, the easier it will be to manage the embroidery hoop. If your fabric ravels, trim it with pinking shears or bind the edges with whip stitching (see Index of Techniques).

Use tracing paper to trace the pattern below. Repeat the area between the dotted lines as many times as necessary to go around your waist. Use dressmaker's carbon paper and a tracing wheel to transfer the pattern onto the belt. The dotted lines should be on the cross grain—that is, the weft—of the fabric.

Embroider the design in crewel wools. For this belt, I used a

The stem stitch.

double strand of wool throughout. To back the belt, use as many layers of belt interfacing and grosgrain ribbon as you need to achieve the desired stiffness. The backing of this belt is identical to that used for the ribbon belt on page 133.

SUGGESTED VARIATIONS:
You might want to design a belt by picking up a motif or color scheme from a favorite scarf to give a basic dress a whole new look. You might also make a crewelwork belt for a strap on a crewelwork bag. Collars can also be stunning in crewel. Work the crewel first. Then mount the ground fabric on interfacing and backing, as in the round Victorian collar in Chapter Five.

Appliquéd and Quilted Cummerbund

A cummerbund has a formal appearance. Its large surface provides the ideal base for really elaborate embroidery or other handwork. Cummerbunds can be interfaced and backed in the same manner as ribbon belts. But another way to add stiffness and shape to a belt is with quilting. Because this cummerbund is stuffed, it will add visual weight to the wearer's waist.

MATERIALS:
　　Heavy cream-colored silk (½ yard)
　　1 green silk square, about 9 × 9 inches
　　1 purple silk square, about 9 × 9 inches
　　Tissue paper
　　Polyester fiber stuffing
　　Polyester fiber batting
　　Silk buttonhole twist
　　Hooks and eyes

TOOLS:
　　Sewing machine
　　Embroidery hoop or frame
　　Crewel needle (size 7, 8 or 9)

This belt is made from silk. The base fabric is off-white; the grapes and leaves are of silk dyed green and purple. The embroidery and quilting were done in silk buttonhole twist.

But many variations in materials and design suggest themselves. For example, you might want to make a cummerbund of needle lace worked over a dark, stuffed shape (as in the coral reef collar on page 123). Couching (see Index of Techniques) is another effective way to decorate a large, flat belt.

To make this design, begin by tracing the leaf shapes on page 140 onto tissue paper. Then machine-baste the tissue paper to a scrap of green silk, using the machine's longest stitch. Use pins to hold the silk steady while the machine does its work.

Use a mug or small plate to trace five circles on tissue paper. Each circle should be about four inches in diameter. Pin and then sew these circles to purple silk scraps. Cut out all the shapes outside of the stitching.

Turn under the edges of both the leaves and the grapes. For the

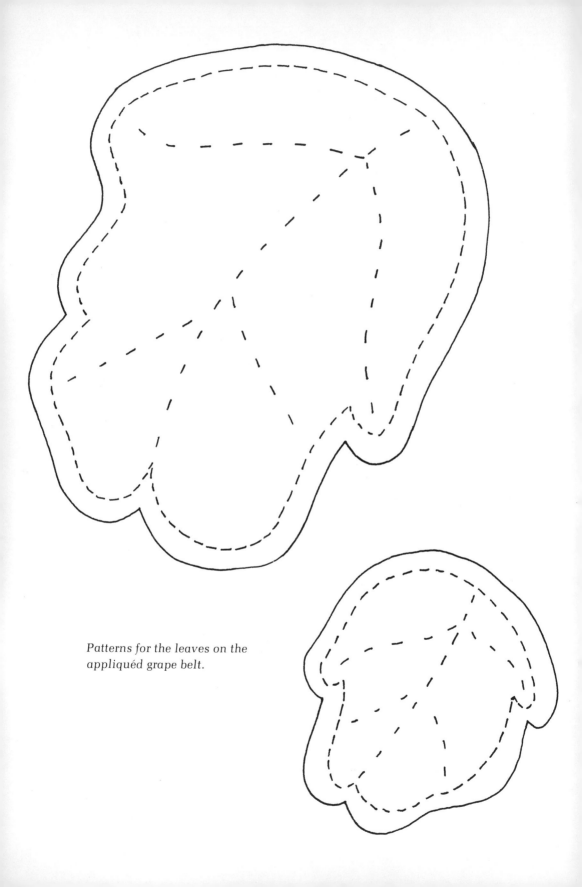

Patterns for the leaves on the
appliquéd grape belt.

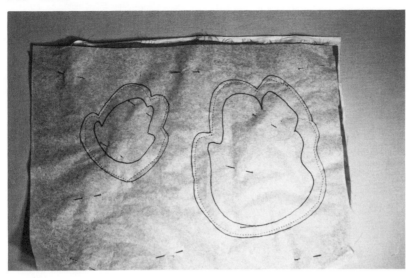

The silk leaf shapes stitched on tissue paper.

grapes, that means making a gathering stitch around the edge of the circle, just as you did for the cloth jewels in Chapter Three and the grape pendant in Chapter Four. After you have finished stitching around the edge, tear off the tissue paper. Then stuff the silk ball and gather it closed.

Turning under the leaf edges is a bit harder. The trick is to make a small clip at each angle, curve or turning point on the leaf's edge. These tiny clips help spread out the fabric as you turn it under; thus you maintain the curves in the original pattern.

The tissue paper removed and the seams clipped. The edges are ready to turn under and appliqué.

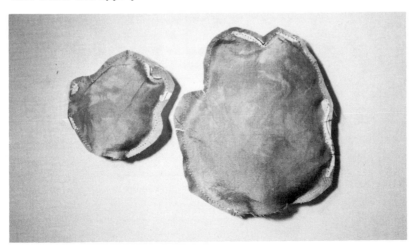

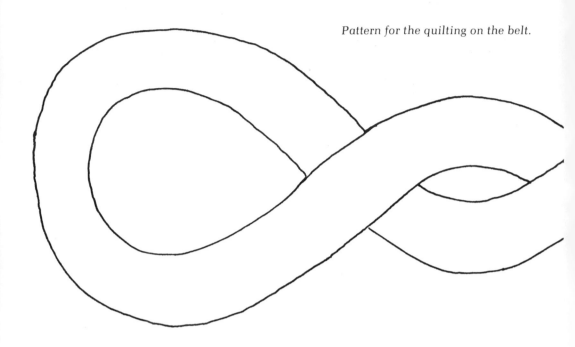

Pattern for the quilting on the belt.

More designs suitable for quilting on belts.

Cut a long strip of your ground fabric. If the background material is silk, it too should be basted to a backing fabric during working. Outline the shape of the belt with basting stitches.

Baste the grapes on first. Appliqué them onto the background fabric with double running stitches. The stitches should show and form part of the design. Remove the basting stitches after the grapes are in place. Now baste and sew on the leaves. Then embroider in the vines, using decorated running stitches. Press the appliquéd and embroidered area.

Next you must get the belt ready for quilting. Cut another long strip of fabric the same size as the strip for the top of the belt. This backing fabric can be any tightly woven material. Plain muslin or Indian Head cotton are good choices. In between, you will need a layer or two of polyester batting. Make the batting layers a little thicker than you want your final belt to be, since some of the batting will get squashed by the quilting stitches.

Next transfer the quilting design onto the belt. The easiest way to do this is to draw your design on tissue paper and then make basting stitches right through the tissue paper and all the layers of cloth. Tear off the tissue paper and quilt right along the basting

The leaves and grapes appliquéd to the belt shape with double running stitches. I used an old picture frame to hold my work in place.

The quilting pattern basted
to the belt.

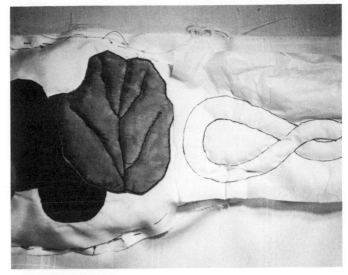

The back and front sides
of the quilting.

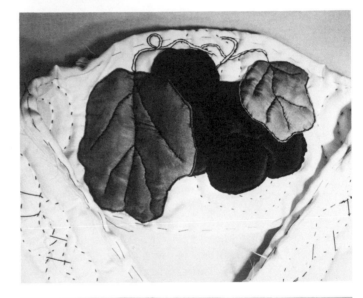

The lining pinned in place.
A small pocket is attached
to the back of the piece.

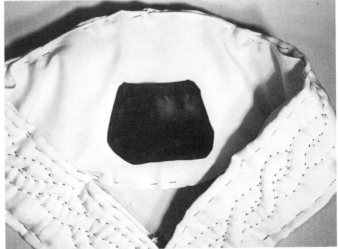

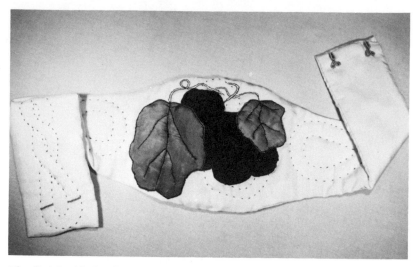

The finished belt, showing the handmade loops for fastening.

lines. The pattern I used for the quilting is shown on pages 142–43, along with some other suggested patterns for quilting a belt.

Quilting is done in small running stitches. On pieces in which the quilting shows on both sides, care should be taken to push the needle through the layers at a slight angle, so that the stitches on both sides are about the same size. On pieces like this one, which will be lines, longer stitches can show on the back.

When you are finished with the quilting, remove the basting threads and press the belt. Use the shape of the quilted belt as the pattern for the lining. Then turn under the edges of both the belt and the lining and baste them down.

Sew the belt and the lining together with slip stitches (see Index of Techniques). If you like, you can sew a pocket into the lining before joining the two belt parts together.

The closure for this belt is another large hook. The eyes, however, are handmade in silk buttonhole twist and needle-lace stitches.

SUGGESTED VARIATIONS:
You can make a more slimming version by backing the belt only with interfacing, as you did the round Victorian collar. You can vary the cummerbund shape to flatter your figure (see Chapter One for directions on designing for your figure).

7 · Purses and Bags

PURSES AND BAGS, like belts, are both decorative and functional. They can be made in a variety of sizes, shapes and materials.

Bags that deserve to be called jewelry are usually small and finely worked. These tiny purses can be worn around the neck, in which case they differ very little from pendants with pockets. A small bag can also slide on a belt or be held in the palm of the hand.

In this chapter, I have included some of the most basic bag

Chinese bag of petit point in silk. Many needle-made jewelry ideas adapt themselves well to needlepoint and petit point. (From Port of Entry, Chicago.)

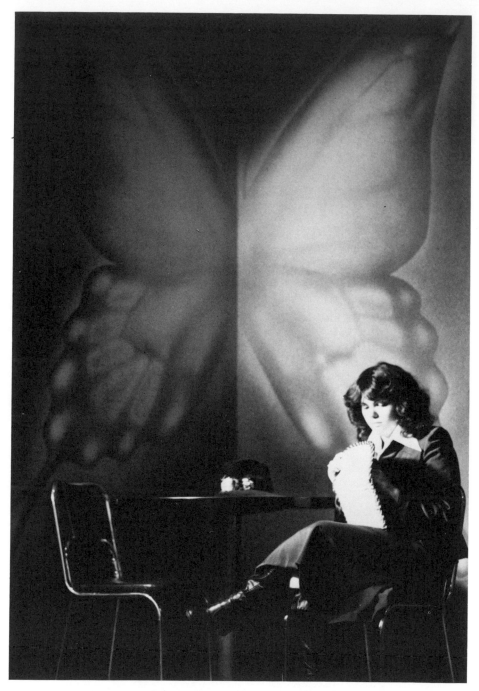

Envelope bag embroidered in blues and browns on tan Oxford cloth and white linen. (Photographed at Le Papillon, Chicago.)

Afghanistani bag decorated with couching. (From Port of Entry, Chicago.)

An American Indian bag (from the Field Museum) with tiny beads attached to the backing fabric a few beads at a time.

designs. The envelope bag has a flap that folds over a pocket, thus protecting its contents. A more elaborate version is the saddle bag, which has flaps and pockets on two sides. The drawstring bag—the simple pouch—is another basic bag form.

Hundreds of variations of these basic forms are possible. The appliquéd silk Chinese sachet you see in this picture is a drawstring bag, as is the Victorian beaded reticule on page 170. This same bag shape can be seen in medieval tapestries and in American Indian costumes.

In making a bag, you should take extra care with the interfacings, seam bindings and other details that add strength. Bags get more use than most accessories. If you make a bag from a light material, use heavy linen or some other washable fabric, and threads that will not run or fade.

Designing your own bags is very rewarding because you can get exactly the bag you want, with pockets just the size for your belongings and in fabric that blends with or accessorizes your clothing perfectly.

Chinese silk drawstring bag, appliquéd in pink, blue and green on yellow, with silk tassels. (From Natural Section, Chicago.)

Ribbon Envelope Purse

This basic envelope bag can be made with rectangles of any fabrics. A lovely bag to carry to the office, for example, might be of brown tweed lined with dark green velveteen. The cord could be made of crocheted or wrapped yarns. An evening purse might be made of brocaded fabrics.

MATERIALS:
    5 strips of ribbon in various widths, each 18 inches long
    Sewing thread
    Cotton velveteen print (¼ yard)
    36-inch drapery cord, with tassels
    Silk buttonhole twist (for attaching cord)

TOOLS:
    Sewing machine
    Crewel needle (size 7, 8 or 9)

Although few people really have the time to work tiny embroidery as people did in the past, there is one way to create that effect of detailed luxury—by using elegant decorated ribbons. A ribbon purse is inexpensive and easy to make. Since an experienced sewer can finish a purse in an hour, it is an ideal project for bazaars and crafts fairs.

The ribbons in these pictures are a wide floral and striped brocade in silver and black; a medium grosgrain in red, silver, gold and black; and a narrow floral brocade in yellow, silver and green on red. The lining fabric is velveteen printed in a red, green and gold paisley.

For a strap, buy a drapery cord with two tassels. Cords like these cost about one dollar in fabric stores and upholstery departments.

Lay the ribbons out on your work table and cut them to the length you wish. The ribbons should form a long rectangle the width and two and a half times the length that you want your finished purse to be.

Sew the ribbons together on the sewing machine (basting them first by hand). Start sewing with the center ribbon. Then overlap one ribbon on the right and one on the left. Sew the outer ribbons on last.

Pin the ribbon rectangle to the lining fabric. Cut the lining to the same size. Now fold the ribbon rectangle into an envelope.

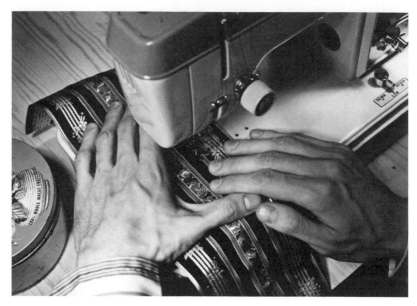

Sewing the ribbons together in strips.

Using the ribbon rectangle as a pattern for the lining.

Attaching the lining with decorated embroidery stitches.

Couching the cord onto the bag.

The finished ribbon bag.

Sew the two side seams on the right side of the ribbons, about one-eighth inch from the edge. Fold the lining in the same way. But sew the lining on the *wrong* side of the fabric, about one-quarter inch from the edge.

Slip the lining inside the ribbon envelope. Fold the lining edges over one-quarter inch. Pin the lining to the purse, folding the top ravelled edges of the ribbons as you pin. Fold and pin the purse and lining together at the front opening as well.

With three strands of cotton embroidery floss, sew the ribbons and lining together. Use running stitches. Make the stitches as even as possible. Remove the pins. Trim the running stitches with decorative embroidery. Use six strands of embroidery floss in a contrasting color.

Attach the drapery cords at the top of the bag, using six strands of embroidery floss. Use the needle to wrap the thread tight around the cord several times. You are making superstrong couching stitches.

Press the finished bag with a warm steam iron, placing a piece of fabric between the iron and the ribbon.

SUGGESTED VARIATIONS:
Patchwork, quilting, embroidery and tie-dyeing all have possibilities for envelope bags. Don't neglect the details on the bag strap. Little envelope bags on long cords are lovely for dancing—even lovelier if the strap is decorated with fancy knotting or rolled ribbon beads (see Chapter Three).

Quilted Butterfly Purse

MATERIALS:
    Heavy linen (12-inch square)
    Oxford cloth (¼ yard)
    Cotton print for lining (¼ yard)
    Tissue paper
    Dressmaker's carbon
    Cotton embroidery floss
    Polyester fiber batting
    Sewing thread
    Bias tape, commercial or handmade (about 1 yard)

TOOLS:
    Embroidery hoop (8-inch size)
    Crewel needle (size 7 or 8)
    Sewing machine

A larger, hand-held purse must be somewhat stiffer than a small bag on a cord. The stiffness in this lovely envelope purse is pro-

Pattern for the embroidery, butterfly purse.

Embroidering the butterfly in running stitches.

Backing the top piece with interfacing. The flap is sewed to the top piece.

vided by light quilting and interfacing. Since the purse was intended for everyday use, I worked it in washable fabrics—Oxford cloth and linen—and used cotton embroidery floss, which is also washable and colorfast. The lining and bias tape trim are also cotton.

The front of the bag is covered by a flap, on which is embroidered a butterfly design in decorated running stitches. If you have more time, you might like to embroider the butterfly in satin stitches, as I did the butterfly in the pendant on page 106. Beautiful effects can be achieved by combining strands of embroidery floss in different colors.

Cut two rectangles of the purse fabric, each larger than the pattern shape. Sew the embroidered flap to one end of one rectangle. Press the piece smooth.

Trace two quilting patterns from pages 158 and 159, using tracing or tissue paper (see Index of Techniques). Make a sandwich of backing fabric, polyester batting and purse fabric. For backing fabric, any tightly woven cotton will do. Pin the quilting pattern

Using the top as a pattern for the lining.

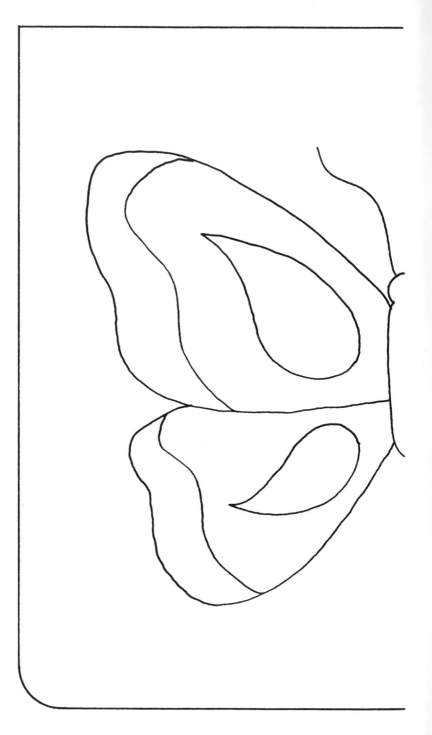

Pattern for the quilting, butterfly purse.

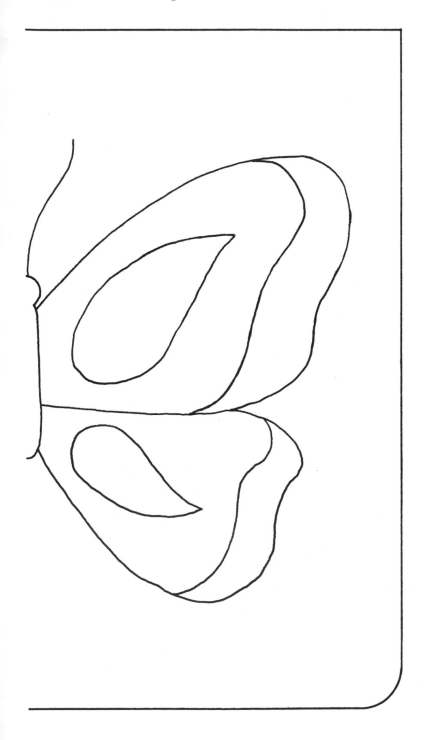

The finished butterfly purse.

Inside the finished purse.

onto the purse fabric. Baste the design through the pattern and through all the layers of fabric. Then tear off the pattern and quilt along the basting lines.

Use embroidery floss to do the quilting. Quilting stitches are small running stitches. As you make each stitch, pull the needle through to the back side of the fabric. Don't gather the fabric on your needle. Quilting is easier when done in a frame. An embroidery hoop works well for small pieces.

Use the two quilted pieces as patterns for the lining. Choose lining fabric that is sturdy and that contrasts effectively with the outer fabric. If you like, you can sew pockets onto the lining before you join it to the purse.

Make a sandwich of the quilted pieces and lining pieces. Pin and then baste all the layers in place. Then bind the edges with wide cotton bias tape.

Making your own bias tape (see Index of Techniques) is really easy if your fabric is cotton. There is no need to baste cotton to tissue paper first, as there is with silk. If you choose a striped pattern, as I did, making bias tape is even easier. Cut across the stripes in an even diagonal to maintain the bias.

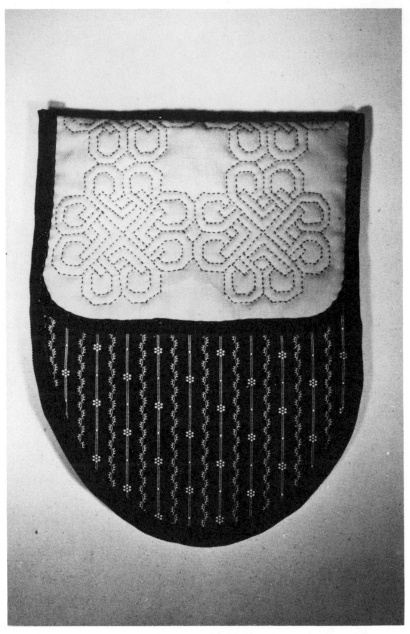

Another quilted bag, with a grape pattern; the quilting and embroidery designs are shown on pages 163 and 164; the finished bag is on page 165.

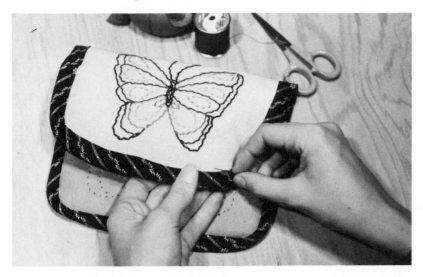

Attaching the lining to the top with bias tape.

I attached one side of the bias tape to the purse by machine and the other side by hand, using slip stitches.

Pattern for the quilting, grape bag.

Pattern for the embroidery,
quilted grape bag.

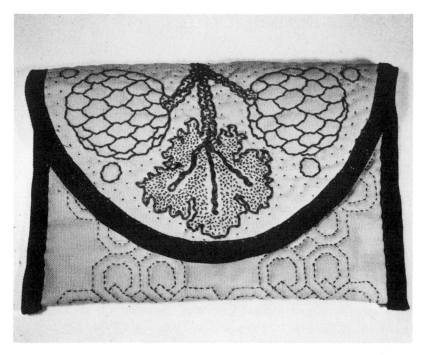

To whom does this design belong? It was woven into an ancient Coptic textile, reproduced in a modern book, and then redrawn and embroidered by me. I chose the fabrics and colors for my project. The original design was woven in purples and yellows.

SUGGESTED VARIATIONS:
Use the front flap of the bag for more elaborate embroidery, patchwork, needle lace or appliquéd forms.

For a larger bag, use heavier interfacing. You might also want to add a quilted belt strap or a strap made from braided cords.

Drawstring Neck Bags

MATERIALS:
   4 pieces of silk in 4 colors, each piece about 5 × 9 inches. Use
      scraps for beads.
   Tissue paper
   Silk sewing thread
   Silk buttonhole twist
   Round polyester cord (3 yards)

TOOLS:
   Sewing machine
   Crewel needle (size 7, 8 or 9)

The pouch is probably the oldest form of carrying bag. Its shape
can be varied infinitely. A pouch can be made with two pieces of
fabric, forming a flat pocket, or with several pieces, forming a
bulbous or globular shape. The silk drawstring bags presented
here are two small pocket pouches threaded on a cord. The
threading system is held in place by large, flat stuffed beads.

   You will need four pieces of material for each final bag, two for
the outer bag and two for the lining. Trace the four bag shapes on
tissue paper. Pin and baste the tissue-paper patterns to the silk
along the lines of the pattern. The tissue paper will hold the silk
in place as you work. This step is unnecessary if you are working
with cotton or some other material that does not slither.

   Place two shapes together, tissue side out, and sew them to-

Sewing the bags together by machine.

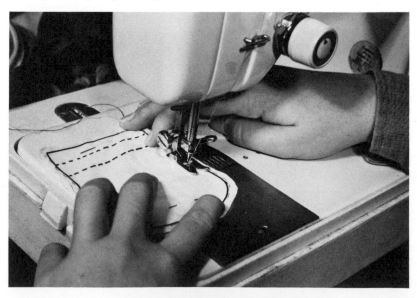

gether by machine. Sew just inside the basting line, making sure to leave openings in the outer bag for the cord to pass through.

Before you turn the outer bags, clip their seams along the curved edges. The lining bags should be clipped too, but they should be left inside out.

Slip the lining bag inside the outer bag. Fold over the top edges of both bags. Pin and then baste the top edges together. Then stitch them with decorated running stitches using threads in contrasting colors. Use these same stitches to bind the side openings. Then put running stitch guidelines where the cords will go, again decorating the running stitches with contrasting threads.

To make the beads, cut six ovals of silk (two per bead). Gather

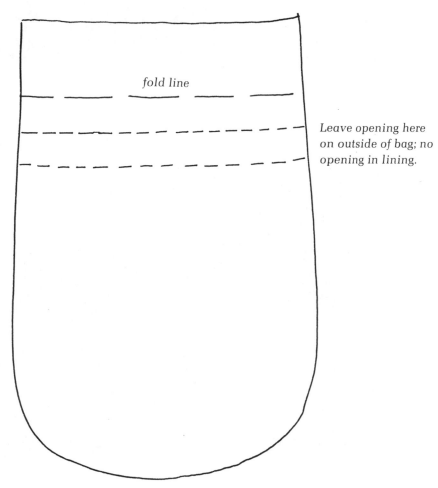

fold line

Leave opening here
on outside of bag; no
opening in lining.

Pattern for the silk drawstring bags.

Attaching the lining with decorated running stitches.

Stringing cords through the bags and attaching the beads.

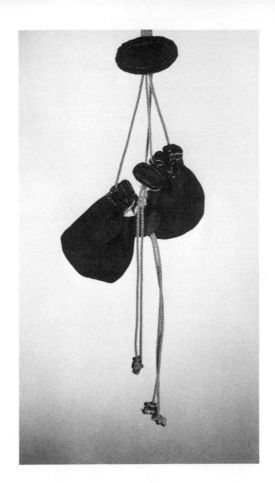

The finished drawstring bags on a neck cord.

and stuff the ovals as you did the round forms in Chapters Three and Four. Put two ovals together, gathered sides in, and sew them together with large double running stitches, leaving openings for the cords to pass through.

Select a cord in a complementary color, thin enough to pass through the openings.

For this piece, I used gold-colored polyester cord. The ends are finished in decorative knots. The threading is done western-style, with the largest bead serving as the tie ring.

SUGGESTED VARIATIONS:
You can make a drawstring bag in any fabric and in any size. Tightly woven, heavy fabrics are best because they will take heavier use. The larger your bag is, the more likely it will need interfacing for strength. But use lightweight interfacing—a drawstring bag should be a soft pouch. Leather is also a good outer material.

The surface of your pouch can be decorated with any of the

techniques used in this book. Choose a lining fabric that is strong and tightly woven and that forms a pleasing contrast with the outer fabric. The gathering cord can be a piece of stuffed silk bias tape, a braid or any of the other cords you learned to make in Chapter Three.

To crochet a pouch, proceed as if you were making a large crocheted bead (see Chapter Three). When you have crocheted the walls up as high as you want them, crochet an openwork pattern (2 single crochets, 2 chains, 2 single crochets, 2 chains, and so on) around the top. Thread a crocheted chain through the openings for a drawstring.

This Victorian reticule was made in the same fashion as the drawstring bags. Its design might give you ideas for a needlepoint or petit point project. The design could also be worked in cotton cross-stitch on a larger bag. (From the collection of David Gordon.)

Painted and Quilted Shell Bag

Small shell purses make lovely bags to hang around your neck when you go dancing. Make sure the closures for both the drawstring and the shell bags are very firm.

MATERIALS:
  Prewashed cotton velveteen (¼ yard)
  Liquid dye
  Polyester fiber stuffing
  Cotton for backing (¼ yard)
  Sewing thread
  Silk buttonhole twist
  Medium-weight nonwoven interfacing (¼ yard)
  Silk for shell lining and pouch lining (¼ yard)
  Silk for pouch (⅛ yard)
  Round silky cording for edging and strap (about 10 yards)

TOOLS:
  Paintbrush
  Embroidery hoop (10-inch size)
  Crewel needle (size 7 or 8)

The bivalve shell is one of the most pleasing natural design forms. But its simplicity is misleading. On close examination, shell designs are rather complex. They involve not only the outer shapes of the shells, but also the textures of their surfaces and the arrangements of their bands of color.

In designing this bag I wasn't concerned about exactly reproducing all the qualities of a shell. The things that were most important to me were the shape of a large shell as it fits in the hand, and the symmetrical bands of color on the front ridges of the shell. After much experimenting, I decided my purposes could best be achieved by first painting and then quilting a shell form.

For the outer shell fabric, I chose a lightweight velveteen in off-white. If you choose a velveteen you will need to wash it several times to remove its finishes. I chose the velveteen because I wanted fabric with a piled texture. Leather proved too difficult to quilt and velvet proved too slithery to handle. Velveteen— which is 100 per cent cotton—can also be more easily painted.

Painting on fabric can be done with many types of paints. Ac-

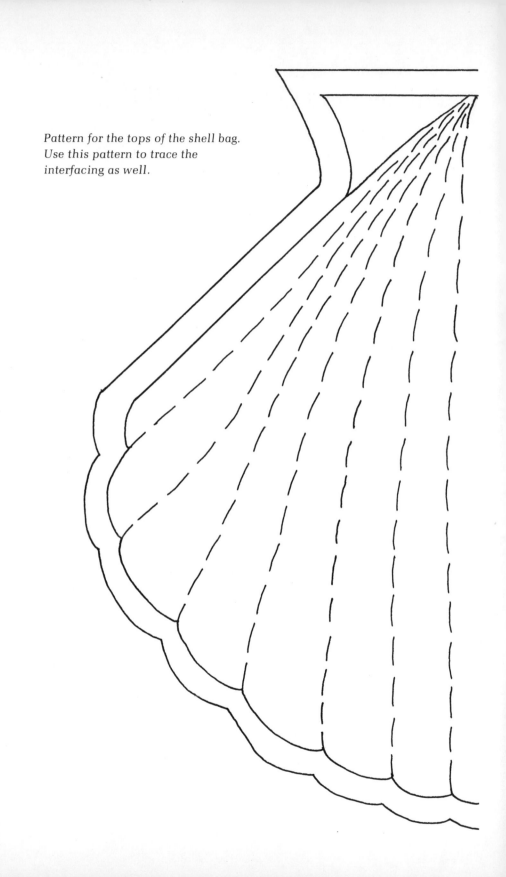

Pattern for the tops of the shell bag.
Use this pattern to trace the
interfacing as well.

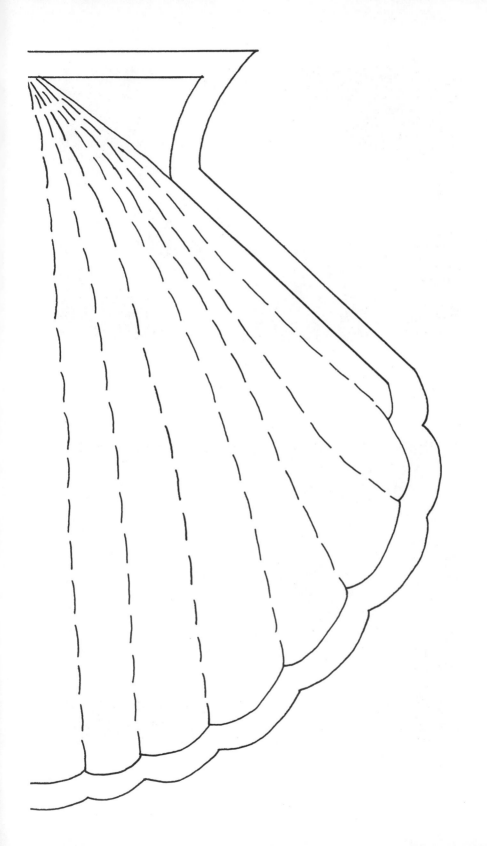

Basting the painted shell onto quilting and backing. Note how the central part of the shell bulges up from extra stuffing.

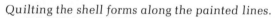

Quilting the shell forms along the painted lines.

Turning over and gathering the quilted edges.

rylic paints can be thinned with water and painted right onto fabric. When the paint dries, it is colorfast and washable. Some types of felt-tip markers are also indelible.

For this purse, I used liquid dye painted full strength onto damp fabric. I painted the design in much brighter colors than I actually wanted. When the dye was dry, I scrubbed the excess out of the fabric. The result is a faded, muted pattern of color. The colors I used were light pink, coral, mauve and brown.

Whatever medium you use for painting, begin by tracing the design onto the fabric. Go over the tracing lines with a felt-tip pen or thin line of paint—your quilting lines must survive the repeated washings that follow the painting process.

When your paint is dry, make a sandwich of the painted-on shells, polyester stuffing and backing. Put much more stuffing in the center of the shell than you do around the edges. This will help the finished shell piece to curve inward. Baste the top, quilting and backing in place.

Quilt along the lines of the shell design. Quilting will be difficult in the middle where you have many layers of stuffing. Concentrate on getting the stitches on top to lie even. Don't worry

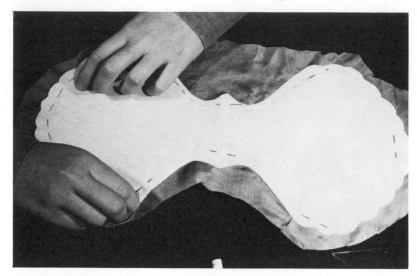

Attaching the lining to the interfacing.

Attaching the lining to the shells.

about what the work looks like on the back. If you make your quilting stitches the same distance apart, interesting horizontal ridges will start to appear on the surface of your shell.

When you finish the quilting, cut out the shell forms, including the scalloped edges. Make little clips on the scallops. Turn each small curve under and baste the fold down. Sew the shell forms together at the top.

Trace two more shell shapes onto a piece of lightweight inter-

Pattern for the soft bag inside the shell.

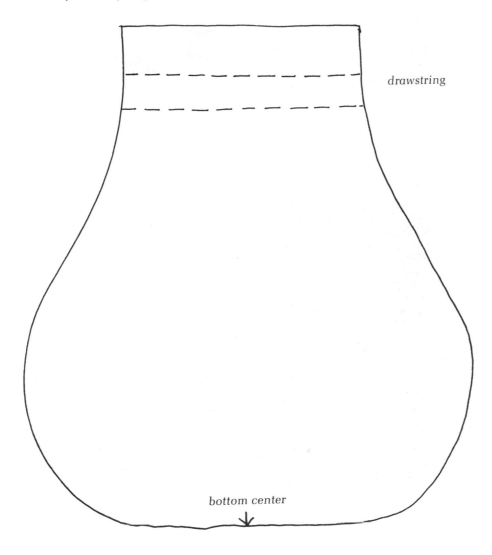

drawstring

bottom center

The inside of the finished bag, showing the soft bag inside.

The outside of the finished bag.

facing. These two shapes should not join at the top but should be separated by about two inches of fabric.

Pin and then baste this interfacing to a piece of silk. Sew the two together about one-quarter inch from the edge and then trim the seam. This makes the lining slightly smaller than the outside shells, further accentuating the shells' inward curve.

Fold the edge of the silk lining under and baste it all around. Pin and then baste the lining to the shells, using small overhand (hem) stitches. Use couched cord to trim the edge of the lining and to tack the lining even more firmly to the tops of the shell forms.

Your lining will buckle at the top, since you cut it two inches longer. This loop that forms will be used to hold the braided handle of the purse as well as to suspend the cords of the inner drawstring bag.

To make the soft bag to put inside the shell, cut eight pieces of silk—four for the outside and four for the lining. Place two bag shapes together, right sides in. Sew from the top edge of the bag to the bottom center. Then place one of the pieces on top of the third piece. Again, sew from the top edge to the center. Add the fourth bag in the same way. Then sew the other side of the fourth bag to the free side of the first bag. As you sew the outer bags, be sure to leave openings in two of the side seams for the cords to pass through.

I lined this shell bag with silk in a deep tangerine color, which was also used to line the coral-colored inner bag. The cords were braided of the same smooth silk I used for the coiled pendant on page 108. This time, however, the cord was dyed dark coral and brown. The bag fastens with a large hook, which fastens over one of the couched cords.

SUGGESTED VARIATIONS:
Make fantasy stuffed forms representing animals or plant forms. A giant leaf form might open to reveal a long, silky pouch in a bright yellow. For a delightful child's purse, make an alligator, hippo or other animal with a big mouth and a huge, slithery tongue. Use cottons and cotton trims to make the purse washable.

Bibliography

THE FOLLOWING ARE some of the many good books that are available in the crafts section of your bookstore. My personal favorites are marked with an asterisk. I have listed the books according to the techniques that they teach.

BATIK AND TIE-DYEING
* Deyrup, Astrith, *Getting Started in Batik*. New York: Macmillan.
Martin, Beryl, *Batik for Beginners*. New York: Scribner's.
Nea, Sarah, *Batik: Materials, Techniques, Design*. New York: Van Nostrand Reinhold.

CROCHETING AND KNITTING
Brock, Delia, and Bodger, Lorraine, *The Adventurous Crocheter*. New York: Simon and Schuster.
* Edson, Nicki, and Stimmel, Arlene, *Creative Crochet*. New York: Watson-Guptill.
Maddox, Marguerite, *Complete Book of Knitting and Crocheting*. New York: Pocket Books.

EMBROIDERY AND NEEDLE LACE
* Anchor Embroidery, *One Hundred Embroidery Stitches*. New York: Scribner's.
Bath, Virginia, *Embroidery Masterworks*. Chicago: Contemporary Books.
Gray, Jennifer, *Machine Embroidery: Technique and Design*. Chicago: Contemporary Books.
Ireys, Katharine, *Encyclopedia of Canvas Embroidery Stitch Patterns*. New York: Thomas Y. Crowell.
* Markrich, Lilo, *Principle of the Stitch*. Chicago: Contemporary Books.

LEATHER
Krohn, Margaret, and Schwebe, Phyllis, *How to Sew Leather, Suede and Fur*. Beverly Hills, California: Bruce.

MACRAMÉ AND KNOTTING
* Graumont, Raoul M., *Handbook of Knots*. Cambridge, Maryland: Cornell Maritime Press.
———, and Hensel, John, *Encyclopedia of Knots and Fancy Rope Work*. Cambridge, Maryland: Cornell Maritime Press.
Harvey, Virginia, *Macramé: The Art of Creative Knotting*. New York: Van Nostrand Reinhold.

NEEDLEPOINT
* Walzer, Marilyn, *Handbook of Needlepoint Stitches*. New York: Van Nostrand Reinhold.

QUILTING
* Ickes, Marguerite, *Standard Book of Quilt-Making and Collecting*. New York: Dover.

SEWING
Perry, Patricia, ed., *The Vogue Sewing Book*. New York: Butterick Fashion.
* Robinson, Renée and Julian, *Penguin Book of Sewing*. Baltimore: Penguin.

WEAVING
* Held, Shirley, *Weaving: A Craftsman's Handbook*. New York: Holt Rinehart and Winston.
Regensteiner, Elsa, *The Art of Weaving*. New York: Van Nostrand Reinhold.

GENERAL BOOKS ON DESIGN
Albers, Anni, *On Designing*. Middletown, Connecticut: Wesleyan University Press.
Justema, William and Doria, *Weaving and Needlecraft Color Course*. New York: Van Nostrand Reinhold.
* Taylor, John F. A., *Design and Expression in the Visual Arts*. Ann Arbor, Michigan: University of Michigan Press.

CRAFT SUPPLIES
Glassman, Judith, *National Guide to Crafts Supplies*. New York: Van Nostrand Reinhold.

List of Projects by Difficulty

Index of Techniques

THIS INDEX will guide you to the techniques described in the instructions. You will find it helpful in designing your own soft jewelry.

Suppliers

YOU CAN BUY the supplies you need for most of the projects in this book at a fabric store, variety store or department store. But shopping for supplies is a huge part of the fun of doing crafts, and shopping at specialty stores can bring you in touch with the loveliest materials available for needle-made jewelry. The following list contains only a few of the many excellent stores in operation. Many of these suppliers operate mail-order businesses. Catalogs and sample cards are available free or for a small fee.

For further listings, check your local Yellow Pages under Arts and Crafts Supplies, Crafts Supplies, Embroidery Supplies, Needlework and Weaving.

NORTHWEST

Austral Enterprises
P.O. Box 70190
Seattle, Washington 98107
*Australian yarns and leathers.
Catalog free.*

Black Sheep Weaving
318 SW 2nd Street
Corvallis, Oregon 97330
*Supplies for weaving and
needlework, dyes and beads.
Catalog free.*

Let's Knot Distributing Company
702 Fifth Street
Oregon City, Oregon 97405
*Macramé cords and beads.
Catalog and samples, $2.50.*

Magnolia Weaving
2635 29th Avenue West
Seattle, Washington 98199
*Unusual and handspun yarns,
macramé supplies. Catalog, 50¢.*

Mexiskeins
P.O. Box 1624
Missoula, Montana 59801
*Imported Mexican yarns.
Catalog and samples, $1.50.*

Robin and Russ Handweavers
533 North Adams Street
McMinnville, Oregon 97128
*Wide assortment of yarns in all
blends and textures. Catalog
$1.50.*

WEST

Colo-Craft, Inc.
1310 South Broadway
Denver, Colorado 80210
Leathers and accessories.

Creative Handweavers
P.O. Box 26480
Los Angeles, California 90026
*Exotic yarns from all over the
world. Sample cards, $2.00.*

Custom Handweavers
Allied Arts Guild
Arbor Road and Creek Drive
Menlo Park, California 94301
*Yarns, macramé supplies,
beads. Catalog free.*

The Dead Cow
1040 River Street
Santa Cruz, California 95060
*Leathers, furs, lacings, findings,
leather dyes and tools. Catalog
free.*

Dharma Trading Company
P.O. Box 1288
Berkeley, California 94701
*Dyes and tools for silkscreen,
handprinting, batik and tie-
dyeing. Catalog free.*

Fibrec, Inc.
2815 18th Street
San Francisco, California 94110
Dyes. Catalog free.

Folklorico Yarn Company
522 Ramona Street
Palo Alto, California 94301
*Yarns and embroidery supplies.
Sample cards, $1.00.*

Greentree Ranch Wools
163 North Carter Lake Road
Loveland, Colorado 80537
*Handspun yarns, looms, dyes.
Catalog and samples, 25¢.*

The Needlecraft Shop
4501 Van Nuys Boulevard
Sherman Oaks, California 91403
*Needlepoint and embroidery
threads and tools. Catalog, 25¢.*

Naturalcraft
2199 Bancroft Way
Berkeley, California 94704
*Yarns, feathers, beads, dyes.
Catalog, $1.00.*

Santa Cruz Mountain Crafts
123 Hoover Road
Santa Cruz, California 95065
*Unusual transfer patterns for
embroidery. Catalog, 25¢.*

SOUTHWEST

Fab Dec
P.O. Box 201
Ingram, Texas 78025
Dyes. Catalog free.

Macramé by Roberts Originals
1934 Prism Street
Houston, Texas 77043
*Macramé supplies, dyes, beads.
Catalog free.*

The Pendleton Shop
Jordan Road
P.O. Box 233
Sedona, Arizona 86338
*Looms, yarns, books. Catalog
free.*

Village Wools
401 Romero NW
Albuquerque, New Mexico
87107
*Yarns, looms, feathers. Catalog
and samples, 75¢.*

MIDWEST
Aiko's Art Supplies
714 N. Wabash Street
Chicago, Illinois 60611
*Unusual papers, batik supplies,
fabric paints. Catalog free.*

Contemporary Quilt
2830 N. Clark Street
Chicago, Illinois 60614
*Natural fabrics, quilting tools
and supplies, batik and
embroidery supplies.*

Fiber and Form
811 Ridge Road
Wilmette, Illinois 60091
*Yarns, weaving and macramé
supplies. Catalog, $1.00.*

The Golden Heddle
P.O. Box 761
Royal Oak, Michigan 48608
*Weaving supplies and yarns,
dyes and batik supplies.
Catalog, 35¢.*

Indiana Leather and Supply
Company
R.R. 2, P.O. Box 103
Bloomington, Indiana 47401
*Leathers, buckles. Catalog,
$1.00.*

International Bead and Novelty
Company
Stephens Building
70 N. State Street
Chicago, Illinois 60602
Beads, buttons, trims.

Weaving Workshop
3350 N. Halsted Street
Chicago, Illinois 60657
Yarns, dyes, beads, feathers.

Yellow Springs Strings
P.O. Box 107
Route 68, Goes Station
Yellow Springs, Ohio 45387
*Yarns, embroidery threads,
macramé supplies, dyes.
Catalog, 50¢.*

SOUTHEAST
American Leather Company
P.O. Box 884
1609 Tampa Street
Tampa, Florida 33601
*Leather, tools, dyes, buckles.
Catalog free.*

Contemporary Quilts
5305 Denwood Avenue
Memphis, Tennessee 38117
*Quilting and appliqué patterns.
Catalog, $1.00.*

The Silver Shuttle
1301 35th Street NW
Washington, D.C. 20007
*Yarns, feathers, weaving
supplies and tools. Catalog,
$1.00.*

Weaver's Workshop
716 Dublin Street
New Orleans, Louisiana 70118
Yarns, feathers, beads.

NORTHEAST

Bare Hill Studios
East Bare Hill Road
Harvard, Massachusetts 01451
Yarns and macramé supplies.
Catalog free.

W. Cushing and Company
North Street
Kennebunkport, Maine 04046
Perfection dyes for all fibers.
Color card, 25 ¢.

Earth Guild/Grateful Union
149 Putnam Avenue
Cambridge, Massachusetts
02139
Yarns, weaving, macramé and
embroidery supplies, dyes,
feathers, beads. Catalog, $1.00.

Fibre Yarn Company
840 Sixth Avenue
New York, New York 10001
Yarns, embroidery threads.

Gettinger Feather Corporation
38 West 38th Street
New York, New York 10018
Feathers of all kinds. Catalog
and samples, $1.75.

Mac Leather Company
424 Broome Street
New York, New York 10013
Leathers of all weights. Catalog
free.

The Mannings—Creative Crafts
R.D. #2
East Berlin, Pennsylvania 17316
Yarns, macramé supplies,
feathers, beads. Catalog, 50 ¢.

Rocky Hollow Herb Farm
P.O. Box 215
Lake Wallkill Road
Sussex, New Jersey 07461
Herbs for natural dyes. Catalog,
$1.50.

Tahki Imports
336 West End Avenue
New York, New york 10023
Yarns.

Tinsel Trading Company
47 West 38th Street
New York, New York 10018
Antique fabrics, braids and
trims.